食飯啦!

eat time!

Essential and Easy Recipes for Ramen, Dumplings, Dim Sum, Stir-Fries, Rice Bowls, Pho, Bibimbaps, and More

Modern Asian Kitchen

Kat Lieu

Founder of the
Award-Winning
@subtleasian.baking

HARVARD COMMON PRESS

Quarto.com

© 2024 Quarto Publishing Group USA Inc.
Text © 2024 Kathleen Lieu
Food Photography © 2024 Michelle K. Min

First Published in 2024 by The Harvard Common Press, an imprint of The Quarto Group,
100 Cummings Center, Suite 265-D, Beverly, MA 01915, USA.
T (978) 282-9590 F (978) 283-2742

The Harvard Common Press titles are also available at discount for retail, wholesale, promotional, and bulk purchase. For details, contact the Special Sales Manager by email at specialsales@quarto.com or by mail at The Quarto Group, Attn: Special Sales Manager, 100 Cummings Center, Suite 265-D, Beverly, MA 01915, USA.

28 27 26 25 24   1 2 3 4 5

ISBN: 978-0-7603-8404-6

Digital edition published in 2024
eISBN: 978-0-7603-8405-3

Library of Congress Cataloging-in-Publication Data available.

Personal photography: Kathleen Lieu and contributors mentioned in the
    corresponding recipes
Food photography: studio iida, san francisco | studio-iida.com
    Photographer: michelle min | michelle@studio-iida.com
    Photo stylist: lizzie oh | lizzie@studio-iida.com
Food stylist: Selina S. Lee | @selina.s.lee
Food stylist/assistant: Yunyi Zhang | @ziraffe_z
Taiwanese food consultant: Linshan Huang
Select detail photos via Shutterstock (pages 25, 49, 51, 53, 89, 91, 101, 137, 147, 165, 167, 173)

Printed in Malaysia

Mom at the Capital Grille in Seattle, 2021

Dad in Belgium, 1973

Philip in Tokyo, 2023

To Mom, and to us, for slowly healing from intergenerational trauma together over a good char siu bao.

To Dad, and to all those I have loved and lost. Though we're apart, you have never, not even for the briefest of moments, left my heart.

To my dear son, Philip, who inspires me every day to dream (and make delicious food for him). How could I tell him to dream big if I don't pursue my own dreams? And, my man, thank you to my man, dear Jake.

Last but not least, of course again, to you (the reader), my dear friend. 🫶 I hope you enjoy all the recipes in this collection: I cook and bake with these every week to share my favorite foods with my loved ones.

Contents

Dear friend, welcome to *Modern Asian Kitchen*, the latest addition to my Modern Asian series. Thank you (谢谢) for picking up this cookbook. My heart is full of love and gratitude, and I'm tearing up as I write this. Becoming a full-time author has been a lifelong endeavor of mine, so thank you for making this dream come true, twice.

It's a dream I've had since the fourth grade. Now nearly forty, but still a forever kid at heart and a chaotic cook and baker, I love experimenting with flavors and techniques. My food is fun and creative, reflective of my third-culture upbringing and early exposure to different cuisines. Take my Pumpkin Spice Miso Udon (page 142), for example, which always brings me back to the pastas and udon dishes I've savored in Japan. Frozen udon, a Japanese staple at most Asian supermarkets, cooks up in about three minutes. Shower it with my delicious "pasta" sauce, easily made with pumpkin

Welcome to My Modern Asian Kitchen

Top: Modern Asian Baking at Home *book tour, Newport Way Library, Bellevue, Washington, USA, 2022*

Right: Family trip to Tokyo, 2019

Far right: Philip's 100-Day Banquet, four generations (Ah Po and Ah Gong in the middle), 2009

puree and miso. Craving some heat? Mix the Korean condiment gochujang or my homemade chili crisp oil (page 176) into the sauce. I promise you'll want to make this quick and easy dish again and again with your own spin, and perhaps, a touch of chaos. ☺

The heartbeat of each of my recipes lies in an Asian ingredient, inspiration, story, or technique, and that's no coincidence. For as long as I remember, while our pantries would always run out of ketchup or Worcestershire sauce, it was always stocked with umami-laden miso and fish sauce, nutty sesame oil, rich soy sauce, versatile Shaoxing wine, and luxurious black vinegar. And just like how I've cooked all my life, you'll be steaming, braising, and wok-frying, while also using your modern equipment like the microwave, oven, air fryer, or pressure cooker.

Where the heart and soul of this cookbook lie, however, is in family recipes and stories. You see, food has always been my family's predominant love language. I often jump to the past, reliving memories of my maternal grandparents, Ah Po and Ah Gong. I can never recall a time when they told me they loved me in Cantonese (I don't think anyone has ever told me they loved me in Cantonese!); however, my grandparents always made sure I ate well. Keeping my tummy full and my taste buds on cloud nine was their way of saying "We love you, Kalay."

To this day, the best work lunch I've ever had was the meal Ah Po and Ah Gong prepared for me when I worked as a home physical therapist in New York City's Chinatown. It was springtime in 2009, at noon, and I found myself without any lunch plans. I headed to my grandparents' cozy apartment nearby on 60 Henry Street. On their dining table was a perfect bowl of piping hot white rice (page 24) topped with steamed *lap cheong* (Chinese sausage), blanched bok choy with garlic oil, and perfectly crispy wok-fried eggs (page 112) glistening with soy sauce, waiting just for me. Somehow, my beloved grandparents had sensed at least one of their many grandchildren would be joining them for lunch that day.

Their heartwarming meal didn't take a whole morning to make, perhaps an hour, with tasks split between my masterful grandparents, who were in their early eighties then. They left Guangzhou sometime in the 1980s and brought flavors from their hometown. Their lifelong love for Cantonese cuisine inspired my burning affection for dim sum (I would have dim sum every day for breakfast if I could), and that's why I dedicate the Dim Sum and Unforgettable Street Food chapter (page 55) in this book to them.

Every Thanksgiving, Ah Po made this amazing garlic oil and soy sauce turkey, enough to feed a family of more than twenty. One day, I'll serve that turkey to

my family (I just stick with a pre-cooked Whole Foods one these days) as I try to re-create all my grandparents' cooking from memory, just like how I re-created Dad's signature egg-saucy beef and *gai lan* stir-fry (page 94). He served this dish with white rice almost every Saturday night when Mom worked as a manicurist. It was such an easy and quick dish, yet hearty and super delicious at the same time. While I rarely eat beef these days, Dad's recipe is still one of my favorite dishes because I knew he had cooked from his heart for my baby sister Evelyn and me. His one-pan signature meal was his way of saying how much he loved us without using any words. (Which was perfect for him, because Dad was the very definition of taciturn.)

Dad grew up in Hanoi. Throughout the early 2000s, on Fridays, he would take us out to eat at a Vietnamese restaurant, usually the one on Avenue U in Brooklyn. (After moving to Bensonhurst, we stuck to a restaurant on 86th Street near Bay Parkway.) He never verbalized this, but I knew he was nostalgic for the food that comforted him in his youth, food similar to what his mother (my Ah Ma) would make, like her refreshing summer rolls (page 32) paired with her unforgettable and easy-to-make peanut dipping sauce (page 168). I'm happy to share her personal recipe, along with our homemade *nước chấm* sauce (page 164), another recipe Ah Ma had passed down.

Hey Dad, if you were still here today, I'd make you all these dishes, plus my version of your cousin, Auntie Eva's pho gà (page 156). While my food won't be exactly how you remember it off the streets of Hanoi, it'll still be tasty and heartwarming.

Unlike my parents and grandparents, I have never cooked or baked in Asia, only in my Asian American kitchen. Thus the recipes I showcase here represent my experiences growing up in an Asian diaspora. They're as authentic as they can be, at least to me. I've also never gone to culinary school or trained or worked in a professional kitchen, so I'm still learning and growing my repertoire alongside you. I will always point out where inspiration was drawn

Top: My family and me in front of Ding Tai Fung, 2018

Right: Ah Ma and me, Montreal, 1985

for each recipe and give credit to the originating culture. Four recipes were adapted from ones by Subtle Asian Baking (SAB) members, so be sure to check those out, including Gunawan Wu's mother's braised and candied pork belly (page 108), Tres Truong's grandmother's fish sauce butter (page 170), Derriel Shine's mother's tinola (page 118), and Meiju Ong's mother's Vietnamese sour noodle soup recipe (page 106). While those recipes were all passed down from previous generations and from a different world and time, they're so delicious and very appreciated in our modern world.

From my beloved neighbor, Mary Usha, who came from Hyderabad (India), I've learned to make her delicious oven-roasted tandoori chicken (page 80) paired with a refreshing raita (page 80). And my good friend Suraj, who had shared a lemongrass recipe for my first book, gave me his recipe for comforting upma (page 130), one he enjoyed growing up in Mumbai and now makes for his family in Seattle.

My mother-in-law Lilanie So Young, from Bacolod, Philippines, taught me how to make a few Filipino dishes, and I consulted her when adapting her chicken adobo recipe and developing the halo-halo recipe on page 186. I'm not sure when my son, Philip, will visit the Philippines, one of the countries of his ancestors, so I'm trying my best to introduce Filipino food to

him. My husband, Jake, benefits too, as he always misses the food he enjoyed growing up, like sizzling *sisig* (page 84), which has now become one of my favorite dishes of all time.

Honestly, all the dishes I share in this book are what I love to eat. They're recipes I consistently turn to during the week to feed my family. Since one of my mother's favorite cuisines is Korean (and she loves Korean dramas and her oppas!), I've learned to make dishes to satisfy her taste buds, like sundubu jjigae (page 102), *tteokbokii*, or spicy Korean rice cakes (page 140), and kimchi scallion pancakes (page 86). Oh, and I've also included a delicious chocolate *gochujang* mochi cake (page 190), a not-too-sweet and subtly spicy decadent dessert meant to be shared. (Of course, you could also keep it to yourself. I won't judge!)

And that, dear friend, is what *Modern Asian Kitchen* is all about: creating delicious yet uncomplicated dishes to share with loved ones and friends, time and again. It's about using food as a universal love language, whether for grand celebrations, casual meals, or those moments when you simply need something filling and comforting. You should always treat yourself first. So, with that in mind, let's roll up our sleeves, kick off our shoes, and get cooking!

Kat Lieu 🤍

Must-Have Tools and Equipment

Here is a list of some of the recurrent tools and equipment I use throughout the book.

AIR FRYER

BAKING AND COOKING SPATULAS

BAKING PANS AND SHEETS

BAMBOO STEAMER OR STAINLESS-STEEL STEAMER (2)

BLENDER OR FOOD PROCESSOR

CHOPSTICKS

CLAY POT

COLANDER

COOKING THERMOMETER

CUTTING BOARD(S)

FRYING PAN OR SKILLET

GLASS STORAGE CONTAINERS (AIRTIGHT)

INSTANT POT® (OR OTHER ELECTRIC PRESSURE COOKER)

JULIENNE GRATER

KITCHEN SCALE

KITCHEN TOWELS

KNIVES (SUCH AS A PARING KNIFE, A CHEF'S KNIFE, AND A MEAT CLEAVER)

LADLE

MICROWAVE

MIXING BOWLS, VARIOUS SIZES AND HEATPROOF

MORTAR AND PESTLE

OFFSET SPATULA

OVEN

PARCHMENT PAPER

RICE COOKER

SAUCEPAN (SMALL AND HEAVY)

SPIDER SKIMMER

STAND MIXER WITH A PADDLE AND WHISK ATTACHMENT

STEAMER RACK

VEGETABLE PEELER

WHISK

WIRE RACK

WOK

"If I could only have one type of food with me, I would bring soy sauce. The reason being that if I have soy sauce, I can flavor a lot of things."
—Martin Yan

My Modern Asian Pantry

Here are some ingredients I try to stock up in my pantry; thanks to globalization, these items are easy to source online, in international aisles of supermarkets, and in Asian groceries.

SWEET

MIRIN: Japanese sweet rice wine for sauces and marinades

ROCK SUGAR: Crystallized sugar commonly used in Chinese cuisine for braising and sweetening

SPICY

DOUBANJIANG: Fermented broad bean and chili condiment, often spicy

GOCHUJANG: Korean fermented chili condiment, sweet but mostly spicy and savory. Check for gluten.

SAMBAL: Indonesian chili sauce, pairs well with noodles and rice

SICHUAN PEPPERCORNS: Adds spicy-numbing heat and depth (or mala taste)

THAI BIRD'S EYE CHILIES: Intense heat, handle with care; resemble the shape of little birds' eyes

WHITE PEPPER: Milder than black, adds subtle heat

UMAMI/SALTY

BONITO FLAKES: Dried tuna fish shavings from Japan, rich in umami

CHICKEN POWDER: Flavor enhancer for sauces and soups. Vegan alternative: mushroom powder.

DRIED SHIITAKE MUSHROOMS: Add earthy richness to dishes, a great vegan substitute for many meat dishes

DRIED SHRIMP: Salty and sweet, great for sauces, steaming, dumplings, and stir-fries

FERMENTED BLACK BEANS: Salty and tangy, perfect for steamed dishes like dim sum spare ribs

FISH SAUCE: Adds umami to dishes, pleasantly pungent, used a lot in Thai and Vietnamese cuisines

FURU: Vegan fermented tofu, tangy and salty, great for sauces and marinades, or enjoy over milk bread toast. Sometimes is red and spicy.

HOISIN SAUCE: Sweet and savory condiment, great for pho and dipping

KOMBU: Edible kelp, key for flavorful dashi and can be used to thicken sauces

MISO: Fermented soybean paste, a staple in Japan; diverse in its uses, also great in sweets

MONOSODIUM GLUTAMATE (MSG): Flavor enhancer found in tomatoes, undeserved bad reputation

OYSTER SAUCE: Flavorful sauce made from oyster extract, vegan versions available, usually made with mushrooms

SALTED EGG YOLK: Strong in umami, perfect in sweet and savory dishes, usually made from duck eggs

SOY SAUCE: Sauce made from fermented soy beans, often not gluten-free. Dark soy sauce adds color, depth, and a sweet caramelized taste. Light soy sauce is often saltier and full of umami.

BITTER/ASTRINGENT

MATCHA: Ground tea leaves, umami and bitter, great in desserts and savory dishes like ramen

SHAOXING WINE: Fermented rice wine, aromatic and subtly sweet

SUBTLE, AND NOT SO SUBTLE

BEAN SPROUTS: Crunchy, slightly nutty, adds texture to dishes

SESAME SEEDS: Nutty and crunchy; black version has stronger flavor than white

LEMONGRASS: Fragrant herb, adds zest to dishes, reminds one of lemons

PANDAN: Fragrant herb, adds a hint of green and a mild flavor. In extract form, it's often compared to vanilla.

SESAME OIL: Luxurious depth and rich, nuttiness, comes in light and dark types

UBE: Purple yam from the Philippines with a subtle vanilla, nutty flavor, vibrant purple color

AROMATICS, SPICES, AND HERBS

BAY LEAF: Mildly bitter, floral fragrance

CUMIN: Comes in powdered or seed form, aromatic and earthy

CURRY LEAF: Fragrant leaves often used in Indian cuisine to infuse a unique, citruslike flavor

FIVE SPICE: Blend of spices, great for dry rubs

STAR ANISE: Licorice-like, adds complexity to dishes

THAI BASIL: Subtly spicy, a little like anise, somewhat sweet

DRY GOODS

FURIKAKE: Umamiful Japanese dry seasoning, great for rice and popcorn

GLUTINOUS RICE FLOUR: Creates stickiness and elasticity in food, like mochi (gluten-free, despite its name)

JASMINE RICE: Slightly sweet, fluffy when cooked

PORK FLOSS: Made from dried braised pork, great topping or filling—try on desserts and bread!

RICE PAPER: Wrapper for rolls and dumplings, practically lasts forever (gluten-free)

SAGO: Clear bobalike pearls from the sago palm tree, adds texture to desserts, flavorless

STICKY RICE: Also known as sweet rice or glutinous rice, becomes sticky after cooking (gluten-free)

TAPIOCA FLOUR: Thickening agent from cassava root, makes food chewy and thickens sauces and soups; great for frying chicken

SOUR

CALAMANSI: Small, tarty citrus fruit from the Philippines

CHINKIANG VINEGAR: Smoky and subtly sweet, great for marinades and dipping

RICE VINEGAR: Mildly sweet and tangy, great in salads and sauces

TAMARIND: Sweet and tangy fruit, often powdered, great for sour soups

YUZU: Fragrant, citrusy Japanese fruit, great in sauces, drinks, desserts

Techniques

STEAMER SETUP

Steaming is an excellent way to both cook and reheat food. It's highly recommended to have a wok, a steamer rack, and a pair of 8- to 10-inch (20.5 to 25.5 cm) bamboo or stainless-steel steamers at home. To use, position the bamboo or stainless-steel steamer directly above boiling water in a wok, ensuring that the water barely touches the steamer's bottom. Cover the food inside the steamer with its lid (photo 1). You can wrap a clean kitchen towel over the lid to capture evaporation droplets from dropping onto the food during steaming.

Both bamboo and stainless-steel steamers can be stacked, one on top of the other. Personally, I stack two on top of my wok and place the lid on the topmost steamer. When using bamboo steamers, remember to line them with parchment paper or cabbage, lettuce, or lotus leaves before placing food directly on them.

If you lack bamboo or stainless-steel steamers, a workaround is to position a steamer rack at the bottom of a wok (or a large pot or heavy saucepan) and fill it with water until it reaches the rack's top (photo 2). Once the water boils, situate a dish or shallow bowl with the food you're planning to steam on the rack. Cover everything with a towel-wrapped lid. The steam from the boiling water will cook the food. Keep an eye on the water level and add hot water as necessary.

In case you don't have a steamer rack or bamboo steamers, here's a handy trick. Mold three sheets of aluminum foil into three balls and arrange them in a triangular formation at the bottom of the wok, pot, or saucepan. Balance the container with the food to be steamed on top of these balls (photo 3). Fill with boiling water up to the top of the balls, cover with a lid, and let it steam away.

WATER-VELVETING TECHNIQUE FOR STIR-FRY PROTEINS

Have you ever wondered how Chinese restaurants manage to make each bite of stir-fried proteins so juicy, tender, and silky? Even in congee, soups, and stews, the proteins always turn out perfectly smooth. The secret lies in a technique called "velveting." Velveting transforms and elevates cooked proteins, preventing them from drying out and becoming tough during cooking, ensuring that each piece remains juicy. The process involves parcooking, which helps trap the flavors of the marinade within the protein. If you have the time, I recommend velveting slices of chicken, fish, pork, or beef before stir-frying.

While there are two main methods of velveting—oil and water—I personally recommend the water-velveting technique. This is because oil-velveting requires flash frying or oil blanching, which involves using a lot of oil and subsequently discarding it, and the results between the two methods are also very similar.

Here's how I velvet proteins:

1. Slice your proteins (chicken, fish, beef, pork, etc.) into thin, even pieces.

2. Marinate the proteins. I recommend using Lai Ching's Go-To Marinade on page 34 and following the recommended marination times outlined there.

3. Bring enough water to a rolling boil in a heavy saucepan, pot, or wok. Submerge the proteins in the boiling water and cook them for 40 to 60 seconds. Remember, this step should be quick since the objective is not to fully cook the protein. Instead, we want to gelatinize or solidify the marinade, which creates a protective layer that seals in the moisture and juiciness of the proteins. This barrier also helps prevent overcooking later. Hence, it's best to avoid eating the proteins at this stage as the inside may still be raw.

4. After boiling, strain and spread out the protein on a paper towel–lined plate to dry. You can then proceed with stir-frying.

QUICK BLANCHING GREEN VEGGIES TECHNIQUE

On busy days when I'm out of dinner ideas but have leafy green veggies like bok choy or pea shoots in the fridge, I add water, a drizzle of oil, some salt, and sliced garlic to a pan, and bring the mixture to a boil. I drop in the washed veggies and in minutes, I'll have a delicious and nutritious dish ready on the table. Definitely dog-ear this page to remind you, and not to sound too corny here, how speedy meals are just a "blanch away!" Here's how you do it:

1. Wash and dry your choice of green vegetable (gai lan, choy sum, green beans, etc.). If there are any thick stems, halve them. Chop up the vegetable as needed to ensure even cooking.

2. Fill a saucepan or pan with enough water to submerge the vegetables and bring to a rolling boil. Add 1 teaspoon salt and 2 tablespoons (30 ml) neutral oil. For added flavor, throw in slices of garlic, if desired, and drizzle in some sesame oil. Reduce the heat to medium, add the vegetables, and blanch for up to 3 minutes. For vegetables that wilt quickly, like spinach, 1 minute is sufficient. During this process, stir and flip the vegetables occasionally.

3. You'll know the vegetables are ready when their color has deepened yet remains vibrantly green. There's no need to shock the vegetables in ice water at this point; however, doing so can halt further cooking and add crispness, which is particularly beneficial for green beans. Once ready, remove from heat and serve with a drizzle of oyster sauce or sizzling hot garlic oil. A bit of sesame oil works well too. For added texture, garnish with fried garlic or fried shallots.

NOTE: For an additional flavor boost, consider adding chicken or mushroom powder, or even chicken stock/broth, to the boiling water. Blanching your veggies in dashi works too.

CHASING THAT WOK HEI

Growing up, I've always thought only Chinese restaurants could achieve the evocative smoky flavor of wok hei, *also known as the "breath of the wok," as coined by my friend Grace Young. It's a flavor that lingers in your mouth, a bit of caramel, warmth, and umami from the burning wok, and always unforgettable and deeply craveable. After numerous stir-frying endeavors, tossing food almost violently, and perfecting my pan-flipping technique, I cried happy tears when I finally achieved that distinct and tantalizing* wok hei *flavor in my own kitchen. Now, you can too.*

Note: I'll assume your wok has been seasoned. If it's not, please Google how to season a wok before you proceed.

1. With stir-frying, mise en place is key. Ensure all ingredients are prepped and within reach as wok cooking is a fast process.

2. Heat your wok over medium-high to high heat. (When in doubt, it's better for the heat to be high than low.) The wok should emit a pleasant, smoky aroma when it's ready.

3. To test if the wok is hot enough, take a small drop of water and flick it onto the hot surface of the wok. If the water droplet evaporates almost immediately upon contact and sizzles or dances across the surface, then the wok is properly heated. While you don't want to burn your food, the key to achieving wok hei is using enough heat while stir-frying.

4. Once the wok is hot, add cold neutral oil, followed by the aromatics such as garlic, shallots, ginger, or onions.

5. Add your protein, followed by starch or noodles, and finally vegetables. Quick-cooking ingredients such as spinach and other delicate vegetables can be added last.

6. Pour the sauce in a circular motion onto the hot wok's wide rims or perimeter—avoid dumping it all at once into the center.

NOTE: Keep in mind, achieving wok hei requires high heat and vigorous tossing and stirring of your ingredients. Pan flips are cool when mastered, but are by no means mandatory.

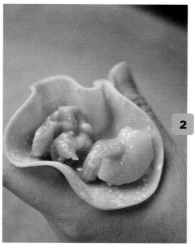

ASSEMBLING SIU MAI

1. Add filling to the center of the wrapper.

2. Cup the dumpling in your nondominant hand.

3. Apply pressure: Use your dominant hand to top off with more filling.

4. Compact the *siu mai*.

5. Siu mai is ready for steaming or freezing.

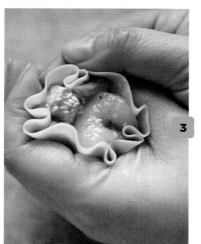

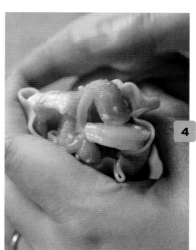

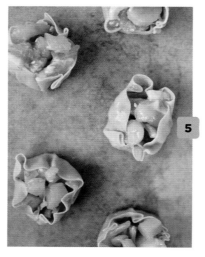

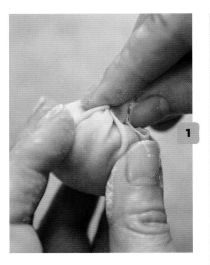

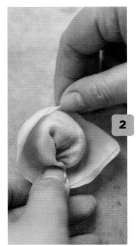

WRAPPING WONTONS

1. For a simple pouch, scrunch the wrapper with your hand and press to seal.

OR

2. To create rectangular ingots, fold the filled wrapper into a rectangle, gently fold down the top, then wet one of the bottom corners. Hold both bottom corners of the wonton and fold them toward the center. Press the bottom corners to seal tightly.

OR

3. To make a pleated purse, fold the filled wonton wrapper into a triangle and pleat the top, creating 3 to 5 pleats for a charming ruffled appearance. Press the top to seal.

Recipe Notes

Unless otherwise specified...

- The first step of every recipe is to gather all your ingredients (mise en place).

- All butter is unsalted.

- All eggs are large (about 2 ounces, or 50 g each).

- Use pasteurized eggs if consuming raw.

- All salt is noniodized kosher or table salt.

- All dairy and plant-based milks are full-fat. (Dairy-free alternatives are listed.)

- Cooking and preparation times are for guidance only, as individual equipment, like ovens and microwaves, varies.

- When no quantity is specified, quantities are flexible and discretionary to taste. Please feel free to adjust my recipes to your taste; I support that!

- Neutral cooking oils include avocado, canola, corn, rapeseed, safflower, and vegetable.

- If you don't have Shaoxing wine handy, use another cooking wine, and black vinegar or rice vinegar can be used instead of Chinkiang vinegar.

- For consistency and accuracy, all ingredients used in this book's recipes, including liquids, are measured in grams with a digital kitchen scale.

- Please compost any food waste.

THE FUNDAMENTALS

"You need a really solid foundation of friends and family to keep you where you need to be."
—Lilly Singh

Absolutely, Lilly! Mastering the fundamentals is the cornerstone of success, not only in the kitchen but in any craft. So, in this section, you'll find recipes and techniques forming the backbone of the book. We start simply with rice, as many of the dishes you'll discover later pair wonderfully with a bowl of rice. We'll cook it to perfection, using a rice cooker or stovetop (page 24). With the rice, we can craft delicious onigiri (page 26), customized to your taste. Then, we'll dive into creating Homemade Awase Dashi (page 28), a staple broth commonly used in Japanese cuisine. With dashi, we'll make a quick and easy miso soup (page 30) or ramen (page 160). Dashi, honestly, can be used in virtually any recipe that calls for broth.

This chapter also includes techniques designed to help you achieve restaurant-quality, stir-fried dishes packed with wok hei (a unique charred aroma and flavor from a well-seasoned wok) at home. We'll marinate and velvet proteins in preparation for stir-frying in a wok, rendering them incredibly silky, juicy, and tender. And for all the veggie enthusiasts out there, we'll blanch verdant vegetables to achieve perfect greenness and crunch—enabling quick and easy leafy greens preparation, anytime, any day.

Finally, as a special treat, I've included one of my personal favorites to end this chapter on a delectably appetizing note—the Miso Garlic Naan (page 36). It's soft and fluffy, featuring a beautiful blistered texture and an umami pop from the miso and garlic. This naan complements all the Indian-inspired dishes in this book superbly, or it can be relished on its own—just like my son Philip prefers.

I'm thrilled for us to dive right in and explore these fundamental recipes and techniques together, helping you personalize new dishes to your liking in no time!

Early on, my grandmother, Ah Ma, recited this poem to me:

锄禾日当午，
汗滴禾下土，
谁知盘中餐，
粒粒皆辛苦！

At noon they hoe up weeds;

Their sweat drips on the soil.

Who knows the rice that feeds,

each grain is the fruit of hard toil!

First, Let's Make Rice

The last lines of the poem above talk about how each granule of rice is toilful. Since then, I make sure to never leave or waste a speck of rice on my plate. And growing up, it always felt like dinner wouldn't be complete if we didn't have rice. I was always in charge of making rice at home, and never once, since the nineties, have I skipped washing rice, so please, please, please, always wash your rice! This helps remove excess starch, preventing the cooked rice grains from sticking to each other, which results in sticky and gummy rice. (Plus, the packaging instructions almost always tell you to wash the rice until the water runs clear.)

If using a rice cooker, follow the manufacturer's instructions. Typically, the water-to-rice ratio is about 1:1 for toothsome or "harder" rice (my fave!); so for every 1 cup (195 g) of rice, you will need 1 cup (235 ml) of water. (Add a bit more water for softer, more tender rice.)

When the rice is ready, and don't skip this step, fluff and loosen it with a rice paddle. Some people swear by using a fork to fluff rice, but forks can scratch the delicate lining of a rice cooker's inner pot, and those aren't cheap to replace!

Now, understandably, not everyone owns a rice cooker. Here's how you can easily make stovetop rice.

**VEGAN &
GLUTEN-FREE**

1½ cups (293 g) uncooked white rice (short, medium, or long-grain)

1½ cups (355 ml) water

Pinch of salt

1. Wash the rice. Don't skip this step!

2. Bring water and a pinch of salt to a rolling boil in a saucepan. Add the rice and return to a boil on medium-high heat.

3. Reduce the heat to low, cover, and let the rice simmer until it's tender and all the water is absorbed, about 15 to 18 minutes.

4. Remove the saucepan from heat and let stand for about 10 minutes, covered. You can cover the saucepan with a clean kitchen towel (stretched over but not touching the rice) and place the lid over the towel to catch the steam. Fluff the rice and serve immediately.

5. Store any leftover rice in an airtight container and refrigerate it for up to 2 days. (Cooked rice left on the counter or stored at warm room temperature can quickly breed bacteria and make you very sick.) One of the best ways to use leftover rice is to make it into fried rice. (Try the Yangzhou Fried Rice with Furu Sauce on page 126 or the Cheesy Kimchi Fried Rice on page 128!) You can also reserve cooked rice for the next recipe.

TIP: *The easiest way, honestly, of washing rice is to add it directly to a colander or fine mesh strainer and rinse with cold water until the water is clear and no longer cloudy. (I love keeping this nutrient-rich water for plants and washing my hair, but that's for another book!)*

PREP TIME	**5 MINUTES**
COOK TIME	**20 MINUTES**
YIELD	**ABOUT 4½ CUPS (990 G) OF COOKED RICE**

Basic Onigiri Adventure

Onigiri is a Japanese rice ball often filled with savory ingredients such as fish or pickled vegetables. While this is a simple recipe, it's iconic and *un-rice-sistible*. Sorry, I couldn't help it. You know me and puns; they're just too *mesme-rice-ing*... Also, Philip told me to add those puns here and to tell you how much he loves onigiri, especially the ones with *ikura* (salmon fish eggs) and cooked salmon. Oh, the easy and delicious ways to his heart! (He also told me to tell you to have a *rice* day, LOL.)

3 cups (495 g) cooked short-grain white rice, cool enough to touch

2 tablespoons (30 ml) sushi vinegar

Pinch of salt

1 tablespoon furikake (18 g) (optional)

About ¾ cup (150 g) filling of your choice: cooked salmon, ikura, pickled plum, grilled eel, or mixed ingredients, all finely chopped (For sweet onigiri, consider fruits, jam, peanut butter, or even chocolate.)

FOR THE OPTIONAL TOPPINGS:

Sesame seeds

Nori (seaweed) flakes

Furikake

1. Stir the sushi vinegar and a pinch of salt into the cooked rice. If desired, mix in the furikake (omit if it doesn't pair well with your filling).

2. Firmly mold the rice into 10 balls. Create an indentation in each with your thumb. Fill this with your chosen filling, then envelop the filling with rice. If you prefer, split each rice ball, place a layer of filling between, and press together.

3. Sculpt the onigiri into triangles (symbolizing a mountain and good fortune) or balls as per your preference. Onigiri molds can help here. Use plastic wrap as needed to hold their shape until serving.

4. Serve the onigiri as is, or pan-fry them into yaki onigiri. Heat 1 tablespoon (15 ml) neutral oil in a frying pan and fry the onigiri until golden brown on both sides, about 1 to 2 minutes per side. Brush with soy sauce for an umami boost. As recipe testers Ingrid and Sabrina Koo concur, "Pan-frying it made it ten times better—yum!"

5. Optionally wrap the onigiri with a strip of *nori* (seaweed)—refer to the photograph for guidance. Sprinkle furikake or sesame seeds as optional toppings. If there's leftover filling like salmon, top the rice ball with it for an erupting volcano look.

6. Serve immediately. To store, wrap in plastic and refrigerate for up to 2 days. The rice might harden over time, so consider steaming or microwaving the onigiri to soften it before enjoying again.

NOTE: *Sushi vinegar is a mix of rice vinegar, sugar, and salt. To make your own at home, add about ½ teaspoon sugar and ¼ teaspoon salt to 2 tablespoons (30 ml) rice vinegar and mix. A splash of mirin into the mixture is okay, too.*

TIP: *The typical ratio of uncooked to cooked rice is 1:3; 1 cup of uncooked rice makes 3 cups of cooked rice.*

MAKE IT VEGAN: Choose vegan fillings for your onigiri. Use vegan furikake.

PREP TIME	**25 MINUTES**
YIELD	**10 MEDIUM ONIGIRI**

Homemade Awase Dashi

Dashi (だし), which translates to "extracted liquid, essence, or stock" in Japanese, is a vital umami powerhouse, serving as a core broth in Japanese (and oftentimes, Korean) cooking. It's utilized as a base for soups and sauces, and as a flavor enhancer for various dishes. When made with a combination of ingredients other than *kombu* (dried kelp), it's called awase dashi. You can also enjoy this as a light, flavorful broth by itself. Think of it as stock (like

chicken or vegetable) used predominantly in Asian cooking and made with ingredients from the deep sea, with the pretty hue of light tea.

8 cups (1.8 L) water

2 large pieces of kombu or 5 smaller pieces

2 cups (24 g) loosely packed dried bonito flakes

4 dried scallops or 2 tablespoons (4.75 g) Chinese dried shrimp (optional)

1 teaspoon MSG (optional)

1 teaspoon mushroom powder (optional)

1. In a pot or heavy saucepan, bring the water to a rolling boil. Add the kombu, reduce the heat to low, and allow the kombu to steep for up to 15 minutes—consider it a mini spa day for the seaweed! Remove the kombu afterward; leaving it in too long may result in a slimy and somewhat bitter broth.

2. Increase the heat to high, bringing the water back to a boil. Add the bonito flakes and any optional ingredients you prefer. If available, a spice bag or cheesecloth sachet can help contain the bonito flakes and other optional ingredients.

3. Once the water is boiling, lower the heat to maintain a simmer, letting the bonito steep in the water for another 15 minutes.

4. Strain the dashi to yield a clear broth. The kombu and optional ingredients can be reused with new bonito flakes to make a second, albeit less rich, batch of dashi. Compost the used components when finished.

5. Use the freshly made dashi immediately for optimal flavor, or store it in the refrigerator for up to 2 to 3 days. Alternatively, you can freeze it for a few months. Keep in mind that the flavor of the dashi will lessen after the second or third day in the refrigerator, so it's best to consume it the day it's prepared. Set some of your dashi aside for the next recipe—a soothing bowl of miso soup awaits!

TIP: If you can't find bonito flakes, swap them with 12 large dried anchovies (heads removed and gutted). You could also try adding 2 tablespoons (30 ml) fish sauce instead of using bonito flakes or anchovies. This recipe yields a generous amount of dashi, so feel free to scale down as needed.

MAKE IT VEGAN: Replace the bonito flakes with 6 rehydrated shiitake mushrooms and omit the dried scallops or shrimp.

PREP TIME	**10 MINUTES**
COOK TIME	**30 MINUTES**
YIELD	**8 CUPS OF DASHI**

Fresh Miso Soup

There are mornings (all right, most mornings) when I wake up in a haze, realizing I haven't prepared breakfast for Philip and it's already 7:15 a.m. The bus arrives promptly at 8:05 a.m. (credit to Ms. Butterfly's punctuality!). As he enjoys an episode of *Pokémon* or *Friends* (yes, my nine-year-old is as much a fan as I am), I scramble to put something together. If there happens to be extra tofu and scallions in the fridge, I opt for a quick, wholesome miso soup. I still remember the first time I tasted this dish at a Japanese restaurant in Montreal with my ZeZe (paternal grandpa). "Try this, Kalay," he encouraged, passing me the miso soup. With no spoon in sight, I cautiously brought the bowl to my lips for a tentative sip—and my six-year-old taste buds sang.

Thank you, ZeZe, for nurturing the foodie in me.

RECIPE SPECS

4 cups (940 ml) dashi (see page 28 for the recipe or refer to this recipe's note)

4 tablespoons (64 g) miso (any color), adjust to taste

Splash of mirin

Splash of cooking wine or sake (optional)

1 tablespoon (2.5 g) dried wakame seaweed

8 ounces (226 g) soft or silken tofu, cut into bite-size cubes

2 stalks scallions, chopped

Sesame seeds for garnish (optional)

1. Over medium heat, bring the dashi to a simmer in a saucepan. Once simmering, reduce the heat to low.

2. In a separate bowl, whisk the miso with a ladleful of the hot broth until smooth. Gradually pour the miso mixture through a fine-mesh strainer into the saucepan of simmering dashi. Use a spoon to push the miso through the strainer. Add a splash of mirin and, if desired, a splash of cooking wine or sake.

3. My preference is for a simple miso soup, typically including *wakame* seaweed, scallions, and tofu. However, feel free to add sliced carrots, *naruto* or *oden* (fish cakes), or any vegetables of your liking.

4. Allow the tofu to heat through and the scallions to soften, approximately 2 to 3 minutes. Avoid boiling the miso soup as this can diminish its nutritional benefits and alter the flavor of the miso by killing off its beneficial bacteria. Once done, remove the saucepan from heat. Optionally, garnish with additional scallions and sesame seeds. Stir with chopsticks, lift the bowl to your lips, and savor each satisfying slurp.

NOTE: *If you're out of dashi or dashi powder, try this hack: add approximately 1 teaspoon fish sauce for every 1 cup (235 ml) water, adjusting to your liking.*

TIP: *Consider creating instant miso soup balls! Combine ½ cup (150 g) miso with about 1½ tablespoons (25 g) dashi stock granules. Compact this mixture into 8 tablespoon-size balls. Press optional add-ins such as freeze-dried tofu, bubu (colorful fried Japanese rice), sesame seeds, scallions, freeze-dried veggies, or dried wakame into each ball. Feel free to mix and match the add-ins. These miso balls can be stored in an airtight container in the freezer for months. To cook, simply drop 1 ball into a bowl or mason jar with about 1 cup (235 ml) hot water. Stir until the miso dissolves, and voilà—your instant miso soup is ready to enjoy!*

PREP TIME	5 MINUTES
COOK TIME	10 MINUTES
YIELD	2 TO 4 SERVINGS

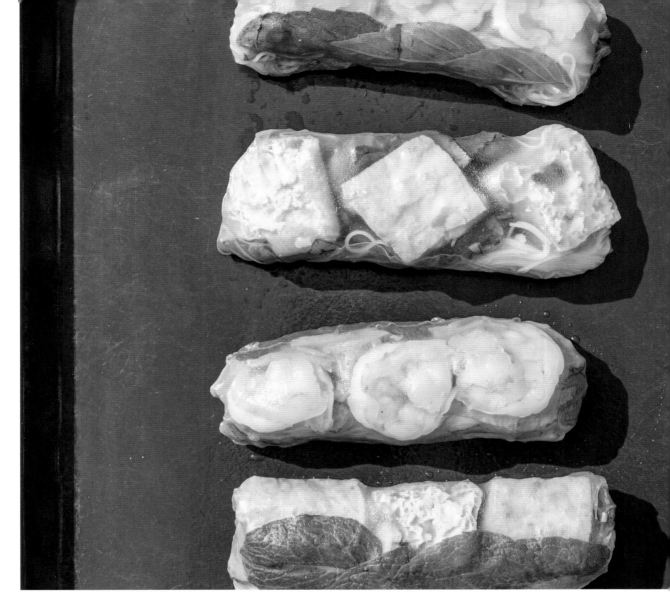

Easy and Fresh Summer Rolls Your Way

My mother and I learned how to make several Vietnamese dishes from my Ah Ma (paternal grandmother), including the classic *gỏi cuốn*, or summer rolls. Her summer rolls were simple, featuring lettuce, vermicelli noodles, poached and unseasoned pork belly slices, and boiled shrimp. Her ingredients were unseasoned because they were supposed to be vessels for her peanut sauce. Usually served as an appetizer, these refreshing and filling rolls often become a full meal in our household.

My recipe here is less of a strict set of instructions and more of a guide, helping you craft summer rolls that align with your taste buds, be it sweet or savory. Recipe testers Ingrid and Sabrina Koo preferred grilled meats over poached ones, showcasing just how adaptable this recipe can be. Ensure you have plenty of rice paper on hand—a long-lasting pantry essential perfect for experimenting with, or when time is short. It can even double as a dumpling wrapper (see page 19).

8 sheets of 8½-inch (22 cm) diameter rice paper, store-bought

FOR A CLASSIC SAVORY SUMMER ROLL:

8 leaves of romaine, butterhead, or iceberg lettuce, washed and dried

About 1¼ cups (100 g) rice vermicelli noodles (Vietnamese rice sticks), rehydrated or cooked according to packaging instructions

½ cup (8 g) herbs like coriander, perilla, Thai basil, or mint leaves (can be mixed), washed, dried, then chopped

8 garlic chives (optional)

1 cup (50 g) bean sprouts (washed and dried) or julienned carrots (for added crunch, optional)

16 thin slices (bite-size pieces) of cooked and lightly salted pork belly, chicken, tofu, or sauteed mushrooms (or pick your own protein)

8 pieces of poached shrimp, split lengthwise in half (optional but recommended, especially with the pork belly)

FOR THE SWEET SUMMER ROLL (FRUIT SUSHI):

About 1 cup (165 g) steamed sticky rice

½ cup (75 g) cut fruit and berries of your choice

Mint leaves (optional)

⅓ cup (80 ml) full-fat coconut milk mixed with ¼ cup (60 ml) sweetened condensed milk, for drizzling

Sugar to taste (optional)

FOR THE OPTIONAL DIPPING SAUCE FOR SAVORY ROLLS:

1 recipe Ah Ma's Simple Peanut Dipping Sauce (page 168)

OR

1 recipe Quick and Easy Nước Chấm (page 164)

PREP TIME	20 MINUTES
YIELD	8 SWEET OR SAVORY SUMMER ROLLS

1. Fill a large shallow dish or bowl with warm to hot water, about one-quarter of the way full. Carefully and fully immerse a sheet of rice paper in the water until it softens, a few seconds. Do not oversoak the rice paper as it may tear. Lay the softened rice paper flat on a cutting board or large plate.

2. For savory rolls, lay out lettuce, noodles, herbs, a garlic chive, bean sprouts or carrots, 2 slices of protein, and 2 halves of shrimp (if using) on the bottom third of the rice paper. Fold the bottom edge over the ingredients, then fold the 2 sides inward, like an envelope. Roll tightly from bottom to top, pressing the ingredients in as you go, so they do not spill out from the top. Repeat with the remaining ingredients to make 8 rolls.

3. For sweet rolls, spread sticky rice, fruits, berries, and mint leaves (if using) on the bottom third of the rice paper. Drizzle sweetened coconut milk over the top and sprinkle with sugar if desired. Fold and roll as per the instructions for savory rolls. Repeat with remaining ingredients. The sweet spring rolls can be sliced into smaller pieces and served like fruit sushi, taking inspiration from Disney EPCOT's frushi! Ensure they're rolled tightly, or they might fall apart when you slice them. (Consider using soy paper instead of rice paper for the sweet rolls.)

4. If desired, prepare the dipping sauces to accompany the savory rolls. The peanut sauce (page 168) also pairs well with the sweet rolls. Serve immediately.

5. Leftover rolls can be covered and refrigerated for up to 2 hours. Any longer, and the rice paper will harden, and reheating the rolls may result in broken rice paper.

P.S.: Mise en place is key here.

TIP: Sticky rice takes about an hour to soak and 40 minutes to steam. If you're short on time, substitute with vermicelli noodles for the sweet summer rolls. Sweetened noodles are intriguing!

MAKE IT VEGAN: For the sweet summer rolls, use vegan sweetened condensed milk. For the savory summer rolls, omit the animal proteins and use only plant-based alternatives.

Lai Ching's Go-To Marinade

Cute story incoming! My mother often helps me marinate meats before I cook them. One evening, I asked her to write up her go-to marinade recipe. She tackled the task just as devotedly as she did when she helped me with my elementary school homework back in the 90s. (Thanks to her, I was a spelling bee and storytelling champion at school!) Mom did a great job using Google to spell and translate some words (other than *chicken power* instead of *chicken powder*, LOL), and I couldn't help but smile and laugh just a little when she

happily handed me her neatly written recipe.

Mom, I've immortalized your recipe in this book, and I know many people will use and treasure it as I do. 🤍

¼ teaspoon salt

1 teaspoon chicken powder or chicken bouillon

Dash of MSG (optional)

1 teaspoon oyster sauce

1 teaspoon granulated sugar

1 teaspoon sesame oil

2 tablespoons (30 ml) soy sauce

1 tablespoon (15 ml) dark soy sauce

½ teaspoon baking soda (optional, though unnecessary for dark meat chicken or plant-based proteins)

1 egg white (optional, but good for chicken breast and tougher red meat to make "more slippery," as Mom puts it)

2 tablespoons (30 ml) Shaoxing wine

2 tablespoons (16 g) cornstarch

2 tablespoons (30 ml) water

1 teaspoon neutral oil

1. Prepare the marinade by combining all the marinade ingredients in a bowl or container. Stir thoroughly before using, as the cornstarch may settle at the bottom.

2. Store in an airtight container in the refrigerator for up to 2 weeks.

NOTES: Add your chosen protein to the marinade, ensuring it's properly sliced or cut first. Massage the marinade in, or stir with chopsticks to ensure a thorough coating.

Marination times vary: Seafood, like shrimp and fish, only requires 10 to 30 minutes. Red meats, like beef and lamb, or poultry, like duck and chicken, need anywhere from 30 minutes up to 2 hours. Pork benefits from at least 1 to 2 hours. Note that acidic marinades can cause proteins to break down, leading to mushiness or toughness.

When you're ready to cook, remove the protein from the refrigerator. Refer to page 16 for instructions on velveting and parcooking the protein before stir-frying.

TIP: This marinade is great for any protein you intend to velvet and stir-fry, and also bake, air-fry, or add to soups and stews.

Mom's handwritten recipe for this marinade, "Chicken Power"

MAKE IT VEGAN: Substitute the chicken bouillon with mushroom bouillon and use vegan oyster sauce. Omit the egg white.

PREP TIME	5 TO 10 MINUTES
YIELD	ENOUGH MARINADE FOR APPROXIMATELY 1 POUND (454 G) OF ALMOST ANY PROTEIN

Miso Garlic Naan

Naan is a magical Indian staple, the ultimate vessel for scooping up sauces, curries, dal, gravies, and dips. (For my son, Philip, it's a treat all on its own. He could happily munch on plain butter naan for dinner. When he misbehaves, I tell him, "*Naan* for you! Ha!")

You can make naan simply with flour, salt, sugar, water, and yeast, or experiment with the dough and add miso and yogurt. It's often buttery, soft, and fluffy with a chew, but it isn't naan without the characteristic blistered bubbles. Achieving those bubbles, as my dear neighbor from Hyderabad, Mary Usha, enlightened me, requires high heat: a very hot skillet or pan.

FOR THE NAAN:

½ cup (120 ml) milk, warmed to 110°F (43°C), using the microwave, in 20-second bursts

1 teaspoon sugar

About 2 teaspoons active dry yeast

1 cup (137 g) bread flour

1¼ cups (156 g) all-purpose flour

½ cup (155 g) plain yogurt or Greek yogurt

1 teaspoon miso or ¼ teaspoon kosher salt

2 tablespoons (28 g) unsalted butter, melted

FOR THE MISO GARLIC BUTTER:

⅓ cup (75 g) unsalted butter, softened

5 garlic cloves, minced

1 teaspoon granulated sugar or brown sugar, adjust to taste

1 teaspoon miso, adjust to taste

¼ cup (4 g) chopped parsley, cilantro, or scallions (optional)

MAKE IT VEGAN: Use plant-based milk or water, vegan yogurt, and vegan butter.

1. Activate the yeast. In a bowl, combine the warm milk (or water), sugar, and yeast. Let it rest until the yeast is foamy and ready to party, about 10 minutes.

2. Make the naan dough. In a mixing bowl by hand or in a stand mixer fitted with the dough hook attachment, combine the bread and all-purpose flour, yogurt, miso or salt, and butter. Add the yeast mixture and mix or knead until a shiny, elastic dough forms.

3. Transfer the dough to a lightly greased bowl and cover with a damp paper or kitchen towel. Let it rise until doubled in size, about 1 hour at warm room temperature. If you're not ready to make the naan, cover the dough with plastic wrap and refrigerate for up to 12 hours (cold proofing).

4. Make the miso garlic butter. Mix all the ingredients in a bowl until well combined. Taste and adjust as needed (adding more miso or garlic if necessary). Heat the mixture in the microwave on high in 10-second bursts to make it easily spreadable.

5. Knead the dough on a lightly floured surface and divide it into 8 equal portions. Roll each portion into circles or ovals, about ⅙ to ¼ inch (4 to 6 mm) thick. Preheat a cast-iron skillet or pan over medium-high heat.

6. Lightly brush 1 side of each piece with the melted miso garlic butter. Once the skillet or pan is hot, place the naan, butter side down.

7. Cook until the naan puffs up and large bubbles form, around a minute. Flip over to cook the other side until golden brown and blistered, another minute. Brush both sides with the miso garlic butter. Repeat to cook the remaining pieces of rolled-out dough.

8. Enjoy immediately with Mary Usha's Tandoori Chicken and Raita (page 80), hummus, gravies, or by themselves, as Philip does. Wrap any leftover naan (if there is any, skip if there is *naan*) in aluminum foil and refrigerate for up to 3 days. To reheat, place the naan (still wrapped in foil) in the oven at 350°F (180°C) for about 10 minutes. Extra naan dough can also be frozen for up to 6 months. Thaw before cooking.

TIP: *If you don't have a tandoor (and that's understandable because I don't have one either), try baking naan in a pizza oven at high temperatures or grilling it at your next barbecue. This recipe makes 8 naan pieces, but feel free to double or triple the ingredients for extra naan.*

PREP TIME	30 MINUTES
COOK TIME	15 MINUTES
INACTIVE TIME	1 HOUR
YIELD	8 PIECES OF NAAN

GARDEN PARTY

"The normal food of man is vegetable."
—*Charles Darwin*

We should pay attention to the man who discovered evolution. And it's easy to do so with all the amazing and delicious plant-based dishes in this chapter. For a busy weeknight dinner, start with one of my go-to dishes, my Garlic Green Beans with Furu (page 44). These crave-worthy green beans are sweet, crisp, crunchy, and full of umami, thanks to the furu and soy sauce.

If you're looking for more protein, try my Beautifully Braised Mushrooms with Ginger on page 42. Just note: You'll probably need to set aside some time to make these mushrooms fork-tender, so plan accordingly. I've also included three salad recipes: One is a Taiwanese-inspired Umami-Packed Spiral Cucumber Salad (page 40), another is my Ah Ma's recipe for Green Papaya Salad (page 52), and my personal favorite is the quick and easy Waifu's Spinach Goma-ae on page 50. This spinach dish is so delicious that you'll want to "*waifu*" (wife) or "spouse up" anyone who makes it for you, figuratively speaking.

If you're not a huge fan of vegetables, this chapter is a great place to start on your journey toward becoming a veggie lover. If you already love vegetables, well then, you really can't go wrong with any of my *radishing* recipes here.

Umami-Packed Spiral Cucumber Salad

Inspired by a delightful dish I had at Dough Zone, a beloved soup dumpling restaurant chain founded in Bellevue, Washington, my perception of cucumbers underwent a revolution. While I have always enjoyed cucumbers and found creative uses for them, such as adding slices to ice water or using them as impromptu eye masks, I never realized their potential for culinary sophistication. The cucumbers in this dish are crisp, packed with umami, and simultaneously light and satisfying. It's no wonder that this salad has become

a sensation on social media. Here's my take on the popular cucumber salad: slightly tangy and bursting with flavor. According to Jake (my forever chauffeur, but mainly husband), "These cucumbers are even more flavorful than the ones we get at Dough Zone!"

2 long cucumbers like English, Japanese, or Persian (but not American), washed and patted dry

3 tablespoons (39 g) granulated sugar

1 teaspoon salt

FOR THE DRESSING:

1½ tablespoons (22 ml) black vinegar or citrus juice like yuzu, calamansi, lime, or lemon

1 teaspoon Shaoxing rice wine

2 teaspoons soy sauce

1 teaspoon dark soy sauce

1 teaspoon sesame oil

Pinch of salt

Dash of MSG (optional)

FOR GARNISHING:

⅓ cup (5 g) cilantro leaves (optional)

2 to 3 bird's eye chilis or any red chili, chopped (optional, though they provide a beautiful pop of red color)

White or black sesame seeds, toasted (optional)

6 garlic cloves, chopped and divided (reserve half for the optional garlic oil)

FOR THE OPTIONAL GARLIC OIL:

3 tablespoons (45 ml) neutral oil

1. Make the dressing. Combine the dressing ingredients in a bowl, cover, and set aside.

2. Prepare the cucumbers. Peel off a long vertical (lengthwise) strip of skin from 2 opposite sides of each cucumber. This makes it easier and more stable to cut them.

3. Place a cucumber between 2 disposable or sturdy chopsticks. The chopsticks will prevent you from cutting the cucumbers all the way down. Carefully make consecutive diagonal cuts (\\\\\\\) at about 2-mm intervals on 1 side of the cucumber. Flip the cucumber 180 degrees and make consecutive straight cuts (| | | | | | |) at the same intervals. Repeat with the second cucumber.

4. Arrange the cucumbers in a spiral on a serving dish or bowl. Sprinkle sugar and salt over the cucumbers and cover. Allow them to marinate for about an hour in the refrigerator.

5. Remove the cucumbers from the refrigerator and drain any excess juice. Pour the dressing over the cucumbers. Garnish with your toppings of choice, adding half of the garlic if you're making the garlic oil; if not, add all the garlic. Refrigerate again for at least 30 minutes so the cucumbers soak up the flavors.

6. To make the optional garlic oil, heat the oil to about 325°F (170°C) and add the reserved garlic. Remove from heat when the garlic is golden and crispy. Drizzle the oil over the cucumbers, making sure to also add the garlic bits.

PREP TIME	10 MINUTES
COOK TIME	5 MINUTES
YIELD	4 SERVINGS

Beautifully Braised Mushrooms with Savory Ginger

Joke time! Why are mushrooms always invited to the party? Because they're such *fun-gis*! Mom jokes aside, this succulent dish of tender, juicy, braised shiitake mushrooms, simmered with zingy ginger in a richly flavorful sauce, might make you the life and fun guy of every potluck party. Patience is needed here though, as the mushrooms take their sweet time to get tender while absorbing all the robust flavors from the sauce. Oh, and don't overlook the ginger slices; their sweet and savory taste brings an unexpected twist to the dish.

RECIPE SPECS

FOR THE SAUCE:

1 cup (235 ml) hot water

1 tablespoon (15 ml) dark soy sauce

1 tablespoon (15 g) brown sugar or granulated sugar (If you have rock sugar, use that instead, about 2 tablespoons [30 g].)

1 tablespoon (15 ml) light soy sauce

1 tablespoon (15 ml) Shaoxing or rice wine

1 teaspoon Chinkiang or rice vinegar

Pinch white pepper

½ teaspoon salt

1 tablespoon (15 ml) oyster sauce or vegan oyster sauce (optional)

1 tablespoon (15 ml) sesame oil

FOR THE MUSHROOMS:

3 tablespoons (45 ml) neutral oil

2 inches (5 cm) ginger, peeled and sliced (into rounds or coins)

2 garlic cloves, chopped

8 ounces (226 g) fresh or rehydrated whole shiitake mushrooms, with the hard stems removed

FOR THE CORNSTARCH SLURRY:

1 teaspoon cornstarch mixed with 2 teaspoons water

FOR THE OPTIONAL TOPPINGS:

Sesame seeds, black or white

Chopped scallions

Fried garlic or fried shallots

1. Make the sauce by combining all the sauce ingredients in a bowl. Adjust the taste as necessary, then set aside.

2. Preheat a heavy saucepan, Dutch oven, or pot over medium-high heat. Once hot, add the oil, ginger, and garlic. Once the garlic is golden (about 1 minute), add the mushrooms and stir until the mushrooms are golden and fragrant, a few minutes.

3. Pour the prepared sauce over the mushrooms. Shiitake mushrooms are like sponges, absorbing water and sauce, so add a little hot water if there isn't enough sauce to submerge the mushrooms.

4. When the sauce bubbles and boil, reduce the heat to low and cover with a lid, occasionally stirring, and cook until the mushrooms are tender. The mushrooms are ready when you can easily poke through them with a fork or chopstick, about 30 minutes.

5. If your sauce is already reduced to your liking, you can skip adding the slurry. Otherwise, mix in the cornstarch slurry, and cook to reduce the sauce until it coats the mushrooms, about 1 minute.

6. Garnish the mushrooms with the optional scallions, sesame seeds, and fried shallots or garlic. Remove from heat. Serve optionally over a bed of blanched bok choy or broccoli, and definitely enjoy with rice.

TIP: *If you're planning to serve this with greens like broccoli or bok choy, blanch them first to create a comfy and yummy jade bed for these luscious mushrooms.*

NOTE: If using dried shiitake mushrooms, about 1.5 to 2 ounces (42 to 57 g) should suffice. Rehydrate them in water for at least 30 minutes.

PREP TIME	15 MINUTES
COOK TIME	30 MINUTES
YIELD	4 SERVINGS

Garlic Green Beans with Furu

One of my childhood favorites was stir-fried water spinach drenched in a memorable *furu* (fermented bean curd) sauce. Each bite of glistening, oil-coated spinach would make me forget about any meat at the sharing table. Water spinach is, alas, difficult to find outside of Asian markets, and cleaning their hollow stems can be time-consuming. Green beans, on the other hand, are easily available and simple to clean, offering a similar crispness and natural sweetness.

RECIPE SPECS

FOR THE FURU SAUCE:

2 heaping teaspoons furu

2 teaspoons granulated sugar

1 teaspoon soy sauce

½ teaspoon salt

1 tablespoon (15 ml) sesame oil

1 tablespoon (15 ml) Shaoxing wine

Dash of MSG (optional)

FOR THE STIR-FRY:

2 cups (300 g) green beans, washed and trimmed

About 2 tablespoons (30 ml) neutral oil

6 garlic cloves, chopped coarsely

FOR THE OPTIONAL TOPPINGS:

Fried shallots or fried garlic

1. Make the furu sauce. In a bowl, combine all furu sauce ingredients and set aside.

2. Fill a heavy saucepan or pot with enough water to submerge the green beans and bring to a rolling boil. Add the green beans, reducing the heat to medium. Blanch until the beans turn a vibrant darker green, about 2 to 3 minutes, then strain. Immerse the beans in a bowl of ice water for a few minutes before straining again.

3. Preheat your wok (or frying pan or skillet) over medium-high heat until it begins to smoke. Add the oil, which will heat up quickly. Then, add the garlic, which should sizzle immediately. Stir until the garlic turns golden, about a minute.

4. Add the green beans. Toss and stir until they glisten, about a minute. Pour the furu sauce around the wok's perimeter (or if you prefer, in the pan's center). Toss and stir to thoroughly coat the green beans with the sauce for 30 to 60 seconds.

5. Remove from heat and optionally garnish with fried shallots or garlic for added texture. Serve immediately. Enjoy every bite—the garlic will be sweetened and packed with umami!

NOTE: *Of course, if you do come across water spinach, definitely try cooking it! For the aromatics, add a few slices of ginger. In the sauce, add drops of fish sauce. Consider topping with chopped Thai chilies for an extra kick.*

TIP: Icing the green beans after cooking keeps them from overcooking, preserving their vibrant green color and crisp texture, so please have a bowl of ice water ready.

PREP TIME	10 MINUTES
COOK TIME	10 MINUTES
YIELD	4 SERVINGS

Blistered Yuzu Shoyu Shishito Peppers

Let's take a trip down memory lane to Blue Ribbon Izakaya, my old Friday-date-night haunt in New York City. The ambiance of the restaurant transported Jake and me to Shinjuku at night, making us forget about the hour-long subway commute from Manhattan to our tiny Brooklyn condo once our date was over. Before I turn this into a cheesy rom-com (more com than rom!), let's get back to this dish, inspired by the soy sauce–glazed shishito peppers we always ordered on date night. Afterward, when I found fresh shishito peppers at Whole Foods, I knew I had to blister them at home for stay-in date nights, with the vent on high and the windows cracked open (or we'd smell it for days).

VEGAN

RECIPE SPECS

FOR THE SAUCE:

1½ tablespoons (22 ml) soy sauce

½ to 1 teaspoon yuzu juice

FOR THE PEPPERS:

12 ounces (340 g) shishito peppers, washed and dried

1 tablespoon (15 ml) neutral oil

½ teaspoon black sesame or sesame oil

Salt and pepper to taste

Sea salt flakes and sesame seed for garnishing, optional

1. Prepare the sauce by mixing the soy sauce and yuzu juice together in a small bowl, then set aside.

2. In a large bowl, toss the peppers with the neutral oil, sesame oil, salt, and pepper until they are evenly coated.

3. Preheat your wok (or frying pan or skillet) over medium-high heat until it begins to smoke. Arrange the peppers in a single layer, allowing them to "sunbathe" on the sizzling pan. Cook undisturbed until blistered underneath, about 3 to 4 minutes.

4. Flip the peppers and cook until they are blistered in spots, tender, and slightly puffed, about 1 to 2 minutes more.

5. Remove the pan from heat. You can either drizzle the prepared sauce over the peppers or use it as a dipping sauce.

6. Garnish the peppers with a sprinkle of sea salt flakes and sesame seeds (if using) and serve immediately.

TIP: *Can't find shishito peppers? No worries—colorful mini sweet peppers, cherry peppers, or bell pepper slices make good stand-ins. The same goes for the yuzu concentrate; if it's out of reach, try lemons, limes, calamansi, or even a dash of rice vinegar.*

NOTE: Shishito peppers are usually mild, but don't let that fool you. About 3 out of 10 pack a surprisingly spicy punch!

PREP TIME	**5 MINUTES**
COOK TIME	**10 MINUTES**
YIELD	**4 SERVINGS**

Fish Fragrant Sichuan Braised Eggplants

If you don't like eggplants (or detest them even, like my dear friend Eddie Wong), I hope I'm about to change your mind. This dish—sweet, sour, and spicy—is a showstopper. Its flavor combo, known as "fish fragrant," hails from Sichuan and comes with its own legend. Folklore says fishermen long ago created this taste sensation, using aromatic ingredients, chilis, and spices with their Yangtze River catches. While there's no fish in this dish, you can add a few drops of fish sauce or even some dried shrimp, as my mom suggests, to mimic the flavor. Of course, you can keep it entirely plant-based, and it'll still be mind-blowingly good. Scratch that—it'll be legendary, and not a bit fishy.

2 long Chinese or Japanese eggplants, washed, with the tops cut off

¼ cup (32 g) cornstarch or potato starch

Neutral oil for frying

4 garlic cloves, chopped

1-inch (2.5 cm) ginger, minced (optional)

1 teaspoon chili flakes or 1 to 2 Thai chilies, chopped

2 scallions, chopped

Shaoxing wine for deglazing (optional)

FOR THE SAUCE:

½ cup (120 ml) chicken or vegetable broth or dashi

1½ tablespoons (20 g) granulated sugar

1 tablespoon (15 ml) soy sauce

1 teaspoon dark soy sauce

1 tablespoon (15 ml) Chinkiang black vinegar

1 cube furu

Drops of fish sauce (optional, omit if keeping vegan)

1 teaspoon cornstarch or potato starch

FOR TOPPING:

Sesame seeds (optional)

Fried shallots or garlic (optional)

1. Slice the eggplants cross-wise into 2- to 3-inch (5 to 7 cm) long segments, then chop each segment into ½ to 1-inch (1 to 2 cm) thick pieces. If presoaking in salt water, see the note. Otherwise, lightly coat with the cornstarch or potato starch.

2. Make the sauce. Combine all the sauce ingredients in a bowl until blended. A few lumps of furu are okay.

3. Preheat the wok (or frying pan or skillet) over medium-high heat until it begins to smoke, then add 3 tablespoons (45 ml) neutral oil. Add the garlic, optional ginger, and chili flakes or chopped chilies. Stir until the garlic is aromatic and golden, about 30 to 60 seconds. Add the eggplants and cook until tender, allowing the sides to turn glossy and golden brown. Deglaze the wok with a splash of Shaoxing wine if needed.

4. Pour the sauce around the wok's perimeter, then fold the eggplants into it. Simmer until the sauce thickens and coats the eggplants, 1 to 2 minutes.

5. Transfer to a serving plate and garnish with the chopped scallions and optional toppings. Serve immediately while nice and hot.

NOTE: *To enhance the texture and flavor of the eggplants, you can soak them in cold salt water for approximately 15 minutes, followed by draining and patting them dry before cooking. This process helps remove excess moisture.*

PREP TIME	**15 MINUTES**
COOK TIME	**15 MINUTES**
YIELD	**4 SERVINGS**

Waifu's Spinach Goma-ae

Growing up, salads were not a typical part of my meals at home, as we usually served our veggies warm—either freshly blanched or oven-roasted. As an adult, I've learned to appreciate chilled or room-temperature vegetables, such as my Umami-Packed Spiral Cucumber Salad on page 50 and this refreshing spinach *goma-ae*. I first had this dish as an appetizer in an izakaya and immediately wanted to re-create it at home. The dish combines so many beautiful flavors (sesame, yuzu, honey, and soy sauce) in a *wafu* (Japanese-style)

dressing that perfectly complements the robust and earthy green flavor of spinach. I like to joke that whoever makes you this dish is someone you should "waifu (or wife) up." Yes, it's that good, good enough for you to consider proposing. (Or, if you're not ready for marriage, you could always just make it yourself.)

8 ounces (225 g) fresh spinach or baby spinach, washed

¼ cup (36 g) white sesame seeds

1 tablespoon (15 ml) soy sauce or 1 teaspoon miso

½ tablespoon mirin

½ tablespoon sake or Shaoxing wine

1 tablespoon (20 g) honey or 1 teaspoon sugar, adjust to taste

1 teaspoon peanut butter, creamy or crunchy

1 teaspoon yuzu or lemon juice

Dash of white or black pepper (optional)

2 tablespoons (18 g) toasted pine nuts or shredded almonds (optional)

1. Bring a saucepan of water (enough to submerge the spinach) to a rolling boil. Add 1 teaspoon salt and blanch the spinach until slightly wilted but still vibrantly green (about 30 to 60 seconds). Drain and rinse under cold water, then squeeze out the excess moisture with your clean hands.

2. Toast the sesame seeds in an ungreased pan over medium heat until they become fragrant and lightly browned, shiny and oily, a few minutes. Remove from heat and allow to cool.

3. Grind the toasted sesame seeds using a mortar and pestle or a small food processor until they're finely ground but not yet a paste. Leaving some seeds intact will add extra crunch to the dish.

4. In a bowl, mix the ground sesame seeds with the soy sauce (or miso), mirin, sake (or Shaoxing wine), honey (or sugar), peanut butter, and yuzu (or lemon) juice until well combined.

5. Add the blanched spinach to the bowl and toss until it's evenly coated. If you like, add a dash of white or black pepper. Stir in the optional pine nuts or almonds, if using.

6. Serve chilled or at room temperature as a salad or side dish.

TIP: *If you don't have sesame seeds handy or wish to skip the toasting step, you can use 3 tablespoons (48 g) crunchy peanut butter instead. Some people like to add sesame oil to their spinach goma-ae; I find that unnecessary.*

PREP TIME	**15 MINUTES**
COOK TIME	**5 MINUTES**
YIELD	**4 SERVINGS**

Ah Ma's Green Papaya Salad

Green papaya salad was one of the few salads I ate at home, mainly at Ah Ma's apartment in Montreal. Ah Ma would carefully hand-hack and chop the hard green papaya and prepare the salad Vietnamese-style, dressing it with her homemade Quick and Easy *Nước Chấm* (page 164). This cool dish is made with love, and each bite is a perfect symphony of spicy, sour, sweet, and salty flavors. Although it's most commonly associated with Thai cuisine (*som tum Thai*), there are different ways to prepare this dish, and it's enjoyed throughout Southeast Asia. Since I don't have Ah Ma's recipe, I relied on my taste memories to develop this dish. *Ah Ma, if only I could taste your cooking and baking again.*

FOR THE SALAD:

1 medium to large-size green papaya, peeled, seeded, and carefully grated or julienned

1 medium carrot, peeled and julienned (optional)

3 to 4 garlic cloves, minced

2 to 3 bird's eye chilies, chopped (optional)

1 tablespoon (2 g) dried shrimp, chopped and pan-toasted (optional)

4 to 6 large boiled shrimp, halved lengthwise (optional)

8 cherry or grape tomatoes, halved (optional, but recommended for a pop of color)

⅓ cup (33 g) blanched green beans, cut into 1-inch (2 cm) segments

Salt and pepper to taste (optional)

4 tablespoons (45 ml) Quick and Easy Nước Chấm (page 164)

FOR THE OPTIONAL TOPPINGS:

¼ cup (35 g) chopped roasted peanuts (recommended)

Scallions, cilantro, or Thai basil, chopped

Sesame seeds

Fried onions, garlic, or shallots

1. In a large bowl, combine all the salad ingredients except the nước chấm. Toss well.

2. Drizzle the nước chấm over the salad and toss again to dress it evenly.

3. Garnish with your choice of toppings—I highly recommend peanuts.

4. Store any leftover salad in an airtight container and refrigerate for up to 2 days.

NOTE: *Hand-hacking a green papaya requires some practice and finesse, so to avoid the accidental loss of fingers, please use a grater, julienne peeler, or mandoline slicer. Recipe tester Judy Shertzer recommends peeling the papaya first, then using the julienne peeler to get down to the center, as holding the whole papaya is easier than cutting it in half and removing the seeds, then using the peeler.*

TIP: *If you can't find green papaya, daikon (radish—slightly bitter) or Japanese mountain yam (a little slimy) can be used instead. And if you don't have nước chấm, make a quick dressing by mixing together 2 tablespoons (30 ml) fish sauce, 2 tablespoons (30 ml) lime juice, and 2 tablespoons (40 g) honey or agave syrup. (Two tablespoons [30 g] brown sugar or palm sugar would work too!) Dilute the flavor as needed with water, and as always, adjust to your taste.*

PREP TIME	**15 MINUTES**
YIELD	**4 SERVINGS**

"Life should be more like dim sum. We should all learn to get oolong."
—unknown

DIM SUM AND UNFORGETTABLE STREET FOOD

"Street food, I believe, is the salvation of the human race."
—Anthony Bourdain

Not gonna lie, writing this book came easily to me because I focused on my favorite joyful and comforting dishes. This made testing the recipes incredibly fun and my taste buds super happy. So, my friend, I really hope you'll love this chapter as much as I do. It's dedicated to my grandparents, who instilled in me a love for dim sum and dumplings. Whether in Montreal's or NYC's Chinatowns, I would always enjoy these dishes: Rice Paper Har Gow (page 58), Sumptious Siu Mai (page 60), and Dim Sum–Style Steamed Spare Ribs (page 68). You'll be surprised at how simple it is to make dim sum at home, so get your steamer all set up and start steaming! For the bakers, you'll get to make two of my favorite savory pastries: my super easy and delicious Vietnamese Pâté Chaud (page 66) and my one-is-not-enough THW Char Siu Bao (page 56).

The latter half of this chapter features delicious and memorable street food dishes, such as flavorful and juicy Tony's Spicy Lamb Skewers (page 70), inspired by those I've enjoyed on the streets of Flushing and in my beloved neighbor's backyard. For something a little different but super easy to make, try my jammy tea eggs (page 72). They always remind me of NYC Chinatown. Oh, and you absolutely must make my incredible and unforgettable Taiwanese popcorn chicken (page 74), inspired by the ones I had many years ago in a food court in Flushing, New York.

So, what are you waiting for? Bet this chapter will have you licking your fingers, and I apologize in advance if your jeans and clothes start feeling snug, as mine now do.

THW Char
Siu Bao

At seventy-two, my mother, whose appetite has lessened with age, once amazed us when she downed three Tim Ho Wan (THW) char siu baos in one sitting. Perhaps her 20,000+ step exploration of Tokyo that day spurred her appetite, or maybe those baos were just that irresistible. Post-trip, I developed an obsession to re-create that recipe, fueled by a nearly four-decade-long yearning for Mom's approval.

As we baked these baos together, she exclaimed in Cantonese, "These are just like Tim Ho Wan's, maybe even better!" While Mom rarely (really, never) vocalizes her affection for me, her gleaming eyes when she savors my food and the joy radiating from her face when we cook and bake together is an affirmation far beyond words.

FOR THE CHAR SIU:

13 ounces (about 1½ cups or 350 g) cooked char siu or Chinese barbecue pork

FOR THE CHAR SIU FILLING SAUCE:

1 tablespoon (20 g) honey

1 teaspoon hoisin sauce

FOR THE MILK BREAD:

1 recipe Queen of the Milk Bread (page 180)

FOR THE COOKIE CRUST:

¼ cup plus 1 teaspoon (60 g) unsalted butter, softened

¼ cup plus 1 tablespoon (63 g) granulated sugar

1 large egg, beaten

¼ teaspoon salt or ½ teaspoon red or white miso

¾ cup (70 g) cake flour

1 teaspoon custard powder (optional)

2 to 4 teaspoons (10 to 20 ml) milk

1 teaspoon vanilla extract (optional)

1. Dice the char siu into pea-size pieces and transfer to a bowl. Mix in the honey and hoisin sauce. (Add more honey and hoisin sauce if it appears too dry.) Cover and refrigerate.

2. Make the milk bread dough up to step 3. Deflate the dough and transfer it to a floured work surface. Divide into 8 to 12 even pieces. Shape each piece into a ball and roll it into a disc, about 4 to 5 inches (10 to 12 cm) in diameter, with the center thicker than the edges. Place 1 to 2 heaping tablespoons of char siu filling in the center. Crimp the edges together, folding over the filling, and seal shut. Roll between your palms to shape into a smoother ball. Place the bao seam side down on a parchment paper or silicone mat–covered baking sheet. Repeat with the remaining dough and filling. Allow at least 2 inches (5 cm) of space between each bao to account for expansion. Cover and let them proof until roughly doubled in size, about 1 hour.

3. About 20 minutes before baking, preheat the oven to 350°F (180°C), positioning a rack in the center and another in the lower third.

4. Prepare the cookie crust. In a stand mixer fitted with the paddle attachment, or by hand with a spatula and whisk, beat the butter and sugar until light and fluffy. Add the egg and salt (or miso) and mix until combined. Sift in the cake flour and optional custard powder, mixing until incorporated. Gradually mix in the milk, 1 tablespoon at a time, to achieve a thick, stable, yet pipeable consistency. Transfer the batter to a piping bag and pipe a coiled pattern onto each proofed bun, starting at the center and working outward, covering about two-thirds of the top of each bun.

5. Bake until the cookie crusts are crispy and the buns have set and the edges are golden brown, 15 to 22 minutes. About 10 minutes into baking, cover the buns with aluminum foil to prevent excessive browning or burning.

6. Enjoy the buns hot with a cup of tea or coffee, or simply on their own. To reheat these buns, recipe tester and my dear friend Jonni Scott recommends wrapping them in foil and baking for about 15 minutes at 350°F (180°C). Uncover the buns and bake for an additional 4 minutes to crisp up the cookie crust. Jonni says, "They'll taste just like new!"

NOTE: This recipe requires time and patience, as it involves multiple steps. To make it more manageable, you might want to prepare the char siu a day in advance. According to Mom, the bun is so delectable on its own that you could even skip making the char siu or substitute another filling.

TIP: To save time, purchase Lee Kum Kee char siu sauce or Chinese barbecue sauce and follow the packet's instructions to prepare the char siu. Store-bought sauces can be rather salty, so balance them out with some sugar and honey.

PREP TIME	**1 HOUR**
COOK TIME	**A LITTLE OVER AN HOUR**
INACTIVE TIME	**UP TO 24 HOURS**
YIELD	**8 TO 12 BUNS**

Rice Paper Har Gow (Shrimp Dumplings)

One of the most iconic Cantonese dishes has to be *har gow*, or shrimp dumplings, often regarded as the "crown jewel or the heavenly king" of dim sum. I've never been able to resist har gow at dim sum restaurants; after all, who could say no to these irresistibly plump and juicy shrimp-stuffed bite-size dumplings fit for royalty? Before developing this hack, I was some-

what intimidated by the idea of making dim sum at home. The wrappers can be tricky to perfect, so I'm okay with taking a shortcut and using versatile gluten-free rice paper as wrappers.

20 to 25 (about 10 ounces or 283 g) medium shrimp, washed, peeled, and deveined

3 tablespoons (24 g) white sesame seeds, ground (optional)

1 tablespoon (14 g) tobiko (or flying fish roe) (optional)

Dash of MSG (optional)

1½ teaspoons cornstarch

½ teaspoon white pepper

1 teaspoon Shaoxing wine

1 teaspoon sesame oil

1 teaspoon soy sauce

1 teaspoon oyster sauce

1 teaspoon brown sugar

¼ teaspoon minced ginger (optional)

About 5 ounces (142 g) bamboo shoots or water chestnuts, finely chopped (optional)

About 12 pieces of rice paper, 6 inches (16 cm) in diameter

1. Line 2 bamboo steamers with parchment paper and grease the paper with pan spray.

2. Chop the shrimp, coarsely, and leave some halved or whole. Prepare the filling by mixing all the ingredients, except for the rice paper, in a large bowl until thoroughly combined. Shrimp absorbs flavor quickly—a marination period of 10 minutes will suffice, though longer is okay too.

3. Fill a shallow bowl or container, wider than the rice paper, with warm to hot water. Working with 1 rice paper at a time, dip it into the water and soak until just softened. Avoid oversoaking, as it can cause the rice paper to break apart. Lay the softened rice paper over a ramekin or cup, and scoop a heaping teaspoonful of filling into the center.

4. Gather the edges of the rice paper together, folding them over the filling, and twist the bunched edges to seal the dumpling shut. The dumpling should resemble a small money bag. Transfer the har gow to one of the bamboo steamers, allowing for about 6 har gow per steamer, each spaced at least 1 inch (2 cm) apart.

5. Repeat the process to create 11 more har gow dumplings.

6. Set up a steamer according to the instructions on page 15. Steam over high heat for 5 to 6 minutes. Any longer and the shrimp will be overcooked and not as crisp.

7. Remove from heat, serve immediately, and enjoy with or without sauce.

NOTE: *If you're up for the challenge and wish to craft the wrappers from scratch (though be warned, they can be tricky to get right), combine roughly ½ cup (65 g) wheat starch, ½ cup (65 g) tapioca starch, ½ cup (120 ml) boiling water, a pinch of salt, and 2 teaspoons of unsalted butter or lard. Stir the mixture with chopsticks and, once cool to the touch, knead until a smooth dough ball forms. Divide this dough into around 12 to 16 even portions, roll each piece into a circle (about 3 inches [7 cm] in diameter), add a generous teaspoon of filling, and fold and pleat into a traditional har gow shape.*

TIP: *To save time, I usually opt for pre-peeled, deveined, and tail-off white shrimp that comes in 1- to 2-pound (454 to 907 g) bags. They're a real time-saver when preparing the shrimp-centric dim sum and dumpling dishes showcased in this chapter.*

PREP TIME	10 MINUTES
COOK TIME	5 TO 6 MINUTES
YIELD	ABOUT 12 DUMPLINGS

Sumptuous
Siu Mai

Okay, so I couldn't include har gow in the dim sum section of this book without its partner in crime, or better yet soulmate, *siu mai*. Of course, I had to make these mouthwatering bites a little sumptuous, topped off with some tobiko or caviar and edible gold flakes. (Don't cancel me, please. I know there are many mixed feelings about edible gold flakes, but I find they add a touch of luxury and fun to this dish, and I'm a sucker for it!) To be even fancier, you can try replacing the shrimp with scallops or even abalone.

Go ahead—experiment a little. The most difficult part about making these dumplings is perfecting the wrapping. Your nondominant hand will cup the wrapper with just the right amount of pressure while your other hand works with the filling. With enough practice, you'll be impressing loved ones in no time, with these homemade siu mai fit for royalty.

FOR THE FILLING:

4 to 6 dried shiitake mushrooms, rehydrated and chopped

8 ounces (226 g) pork collar (the fattier, the better), diced

20 to 25 (about 10 ounces or 283 g) medium shrimp, washed, peeled, deveined, and coarsely chopped

½ teaspoon minced ginger (optional)

½ teaspoon kosher salt

1½ teaspoons sugar

1 teaspoon Shaoxing wine

2 teaspoons cornstarch

1 tablespoon (15 ml) sesame oil

Dash of MSG (optional)

1 teaspoon chicken or mushroom bouillon powder (optional)

1 tablespoon (15 ml) soy sauce

1 tablespoon (15 ml) oyster sauce (optional)

½ teaspoon white pepper

Up to 1 tablespoon (15 g) lard or duck fat (optional)

1 egg white to serve as a binder

FOR WRAPPING:

20 to 21 circular and thin wonton wrappers or Hong Kong–style siu mai wrappers

FOR THE OPTIONAL TOPPINGS:

Goji berries

Any color tobiko or caviar

Edamame or peas

Grated carrots

Edible gold flakes

PREP TIME	30 TO 45 MINUTES
COOK TIME	7 MINUTES
INACTIVE TIME	30 MINUTES
YIELD	ABOUT 20 TO 21 SIU MAI

1. Combine all the filling ingredients thoroughly in a bowl. Cover and refrigerate for at least 30 minutes.

2. Assemble the siu mai (see page 19). Add a heaping teaspoonful of filling to the center of the wrapper. Use a butter knife (or frosting spatula) to spread the filling in an even layer, leaving about an ⅛-inch (3 mm) border. Form an "O" shape with the thumb and index finger of your nondominant hand and cup the filled wrapper. Apply pressure with your thumb and index finger. Pleats should form as you cup the wrapper. Add a little more filling with the butter knife (this is an open-faced dumpling) and level off the top, pushing down the filling while applying even and firm pressure with your thumb and index finger. (Don't squeeze too hard or the filling will pop out, but squeeze hard enough so the wrapper sticks to the filling.) There should be no air bubbles or space between the wrapping and the filling. Gently flatten the bottom of the dumpling with your finger, and press in the pleats/folds around the siu mai, as needed. Repeat to assemble 19 to 20 more dumplings. "The forming takes practice, but not for lack of instructions," recipe tester Chi Nguyen points out.

3. Top each siu mai with a goji berry and/or about a ¼ teaspoon tobiko or caviar. Alternatively, top each with an edamame or pea, or grated carrots. Feel free to mix things up!

4. Set up a steamer according to the instructions on page 15. Steam about 10 siu mai at a time, or in smaller batches, over high heat until the filling is cooked through and the wrappers glisten, 6 to 7 minutes.

5. Top with edible gold flakes if you'd like. Serve immediately, with your sauces of choice. I like them sans sauce, but sometimes also with a little red vinegar and *Fire* Chili Crisp Oil (page 176).

NOTE: *With most dumplings, you can place assembled, uncooked ones on a tray in a single layer and freeze them, uncovered, for about 1 hour. (Recipe tester Mindy Cheung used muffin pans for this.) Once frozen, transfer to storage bags or containers and store in the freezer for up to 6 months (or longer, really). To cook frozen dumplings, steam them, unthawed, for about 10 to 12 minutes.*

MAKE IT VEGAN: *To make about 18 ounces (510 g) of filling total, here's a general guide: Mix together 5 ounces (142 g) soft tofu or steamed taro; 4 ounces (113 g) each of edamame, peas, and carrots; and 3 ounces (85 g) shiitake mushrooms. Add the same seasoning/marinade as described in the main recipe. You can also include wood ear mushrooms or chopped snow pea shoots for extra texture. Skip the lard and use vegan oyster sauce. Vegan wonton wrappers are available by Nasoya and NUCO.*

NOTE: As this recipe yields about 100 wontons, consider enlisting a family member or friend to join you in this enjoyable activity. Mom and I teamed up and prepared 100 fresh wontons in under 30 minutes!

100 Dreams of Toronto Wontons

In Chinese, "wonton" translates to "cloud swallowing," something I just realized as an adult, and a concept I never quite grasped. The wontons I adore are Hong Kong–style, plump, filled with crisp shrimp, and incredibly satisfying, reminiscent of those I enjoyed during my childhood in Toronto. Served with a drizzle of red vinegar and accompanied by a simple broth and egg noodles, they were divine. Perhaps that's the origin of their name, offering a little taste of paradise with each bite, an ethereal puff of cloudlike taste in your mouth.

This particular wonton recipe is inspired by Subtle Asian Baking member and recipe tester Ingrid Koo, who frequently delivered freshly made wonton soup to friends quarantining or isolating themselves during the COVID-19 pandemic. Her wontons were so well-loved that she began documenting her recipes, compiling a collection for her son, Matthew, to use in his college dorm. Ingrid, thank you for sharing your delightful recipe with me!

FOR THE WONTON FILLING:

1 pound (454 g) Kurobuta or fatty ground pork

20 to 25 (10 ounces or 283 g) medium shrimp, washed, peeled, deveined, and chopped coarsely

4 gai lan (Chinese broccoli) stems, chopped finely, or 6 ounces (170 g) water chestnuts, chopped (optional, for added crunch)

A small bunch of Chinese yellow chives, chopped finely (optional but highly recommended)

1 egg, beaten

3 tablespoons (45 ml) Shaoxing wine

1½ tablespoons (22 ml) soy sauce

2 tablespoons (30 ml) oyster sauce

1 tablespoon (15 ml) sesame oil

1 teaspoon fish sauce

1 teaspoon dried flounder powder or hondashi powder (optional)

1 teaspoon white pepper

1 teaspoon kosher salt, adjust to taste

1½ teaspoons granulated sugar

3 tablespoons (24 g) white sesame, ground into a powder

Dash of MSG

½ teaspoon chicken or mushroom bouillon powder

2 teaspoons cornstarch or potato starch

FOR THE WONTON WRAPPERS:

100 Hong Kong or Chinese thin wonton wrappers

1 beaten egg or some water

FOR THE OPTIONAL SAUCE:

1 recipe Kat's Everyday Dipping Sauce (page 166)

1 recipe *Fire* Chili Crisp Oil (page 176)

PREP TIME	30 MINUTES
COOK TIME	5 MINUTES
YIELD	ABOUT 100 WONTONS

1. Combine all wonton filling ingredients in a large bowl, using a spatula, chopsticks, or clean hands, until the filling achieves a "stringlike appearance," as Ingrid describes it, or is thoroughly mixed. Refrigerate the filling for 30 minutes or overnight.

2. Place 1 wonton wrapper in the center of your work surface. Add about 1 teaspoon of filling to the wrapper's center. Moisten a clean fingertip with beaten egg or water and brush around the wrapper's edges. There are several ways to wrap wontons. Refer to the wonton wrapping technique on page 20 for three methods.

3. Arrange the wontons with a small gap between each on a baking sheet if you wish to freeze and store them. Once frozen, transfer the wontons to a freezer storage bag or container.

4. To cook the wontons, bring a pot of water to a rolling boil (consider adding a splash of sesame oil, soy sauce, and vinegar to the water). Carefully drop in the wontons and cook over medium-high heat. Once the wontons float to the top, they are typically ready, 3 to 4 minutes (or 6 to 7 minutes when frozen). Note that wontons can also be cooked in broth. (I prefer this, as it adds flavor to the wontons.)

5. Prepare my optional dipping sauce and chili crisp oil. Strain the wontons and serve with the sauce and chili crisp oil, if desired.

TIP: For a crispy alternative, these wontons can be deep-fried in oil that's heated to about 350°F (180°C) until golden brown all over and floating in the oil, a few minutes. P.S.: Nothing is stopping you from pan-frying these wontons!

Ingrid and Sabrina Koo

TIP: The glutinous rice can be cooked first before adding it to the packages, which recipe tester Judy Shertzer recommends, as it makes the parcels easier to wrap. If that's the case, the packages will only need about 20 minutes of steaming instead of 90. It'll still take time to precook the rice, at least 40 minutes in a steamer, and less time in a microwave (please Google how to cook sticky rice in a microwave).

Lotus Leaf–Wrapped Sticky Rice (Lo Mai Gai)

With this labor-of-love and step-intensive recipe, mise en place is key for success. Definitely read through the recipe first (there's soaking, precooking, a long steaming period). Also, it's okay if you can't find lotus leaves. While they add a subtle sweetness, fragrance, and pleasing aesthetic to this dish, parchment-wrapped sticky rice will come out just as good.

Usually, we enjoy *lo mai gai* as dim sum; the portions here are big and satisfying enough to serve as an entrée. Just don't start making this dish on a hectic weeknight and expect it ready for dinner the same night.

2 cups (380 g) uncooked glutinous rice (sticky rice), washed thoroughly and soaked in water for at least 1 hour

2 large dried lotus leaves, cut in half down the middle and soaked for an hour in water or 4 large (2-foot [61 cm] long) pieces of parchment paper (not wax paper)

Kitchen twine

FOR THE MARINATED CHICKEN:

½ to 1 pound (226 to 454 g) boneless chicken-thigh or drumstick meat, cubed or sliced (bite-size)

1 recipe Lai Ching's Go-To Marinade (page 34)

FOR THE RICE SEASONING:

¼ teaspoon five-spice powder

1 tablespoon (15 ml) oyster sauce

1 tablespoon (15 ml) sesame oil

1 teaspoon Shaoxing wine

½ teaspoon sugar

1 tablespoon (15 ml) dark soy sauce

Dash of white pepper (optional)

Dash of MSG (optional)

1 teaspoon chicken bouillon powder (optional)

FOR THE ADDITIONAL FILLINGS:

Neutral oil

2 to 3 garlic cloves, minced

1 shallot, minced

6 to 8 dried shiitake mushrooms, rehydrated and sliced

2 tablespoons (5 g) small dried shrimp, soaked in water for 15 minutes, drained, and chopped (optional)

1 to 2 pieces of dried scallop, soaked in water for 15 minutes (optional)

2 *lap cheong* (Chinese sausages) or 2 ounces (28 g) *lap yuk* (Chinese bacon), or 1 to 2 ounces (14 to 28 g) Chinese Barbecue Pork (page 96), chopped into bite-size slices or pieces (optional and you can mix and match)

2 salted duck egg yolks, halved (optional, but recommended)

PREP TIME	20 MINUTES
COOK TIME	1 HOUR 55 MINUTES
INACTIVE TIME	2 HOURS TO OVERNIGHT
YIELD	4 LARGE LOTUS LEAF–WRAPPED STICKY RICE PACKAGES

1. Marinate the chicken. Make 1 recipe Lai Ching's marinade in a bowl or container and add the chicken. Massage in the marinade, or stir with chopsticks to fully coat everything. Cover and set aside in the refrigerator for at least 30 minutes before cooking.

2. Make the rice seasoning by combining all the rice seasoning ingredients in a small bowl. Give it a taste to see if it's to your liking, adjust as needed, then cover and set aside.

3. Sauté the filling ingredients. Add 1 to 2 tablespoons (15 to 30 ml) neutral oil to coat the wok or pan before tossing in the garlic, shallot, and mushrooms. Cook until the mushrooms are golden, a few minutes. Add the dried shrimp and dried scallop, if using. Stir-fry and toss everything until aromatic and shiny, a few minutes, then remove from heat and set aside in a large bowl.

4. Cook the chicken. In the same wok or pan, add 2 tablespoons (30 ml) neutral oil and toss in the marinated chicken. Cook over high heat until all sides are golden brown, a few minutes. Remove from heat and set aside.

5. Drain the soaked rice and add it to the bowl with the sauteed filling ingredients. Stir in the rice seasoning to thoroughly combine into a sticky rice mixture.

6. Assemble the lotus leaf wraps. The lotus leaves should be drained and dried. Lay flat on a clean work surface. Alternatively, use 4 pieces of parchment paper. Place about ½ cup (98 g) (uncooked) sticky rice mixture in the center of each lotus leaf or parchment paper, and flatten into a 5 x 5-inch (13 x 13-cm) square. (Add more than ½ cup [98 g] of sticky rice mixture at a time if you had precooked the rice.) Add a few spoonfuls of the cooked chicken, optional pork toppings (lap cheong, lap yuk, and/or char siu), and one half of a salted duck yolk. Spread the ingredients evenly on top of the rice mixture square. Top with another ½ cup (98 g) uncooked sticky rice mixture (more if using cooked rice), spreading it out to cover the meats and egg yolk.

7. Wrap the packages by folding the edges of the lotus leaf or parchment paper around the filling, packed tightly, to form an adorable squarish package. Use the kitchen twine to securely tie the package. You can wrap it just once around or like a present. Repeat steps 6 and 7 to assemble 3 more packages.

8. Set up a steamer according to the instructions on page 15 and steam the packages over medium-high heat for about 90 minutes.

9. Remove from heat, remove the twine carefully, serve hot, and enjoy! A little *Fire* Chili Crisp Oil (page 176) goes well with this dish.

Pâté Chaud
(Bánh Patê Sô)

Diving deep into the history of *pâté chaud* (also known as *bánh patê sô* or Vietnamese hot meat pie), we can trace its origins back to the French colonization of Vietnam, much like the bánh mì sandwich. French bakers introduced European-style pastries to the local population, catering to the palates of the colonizers who sought to maintain their European diets and eating habits. I won't delve into the complex history of colonization and food in this context, as it's quite an extensive and dark subject.

But as someone who grew up half-Vietnamese, I've always been fond of pâté chaud and have appreciated its cultural significance to the people of Vietnam. Not only does it hold an important place in Vietnamese cuisine, it's also incredibly delicious! The buttery, flaky pastry encases juicy bites of fish sauce–flavored pork and liver pâté.

Liver pâté can be challenging to find; I recall one night when I visited two different supermarkets without any luck. If you can't find liver pâté, you can substitute it with mushroom pâté or sesame paste, as I've done here, or simply omit it altogether. The tahini will impart slight bitterness, and recipe tester Susan Louangsaysongkham and her family prefer their pâté chaud without it. (I enjoy the bitterness.)

FOR THE FILLING:

Neutral oil

1 medium onion, minced

4 garlic cloves, minced

2 tablespoons (32 g) Chinese sesame paste or tahini (optional)

1 pound (453 g) fatty ground pork or plant-based minced meat, like Impossible Foods

2 tablespoons (30 ml) fish sauce

1 tablespoon (15 ml) oyster sauce

1 tablespoon (15 ml) Shaoxing wine

1 teaspoon soy sauce

1 tablespoon (8 g) cornstarch

½ teaspoon ground black pepper

1 teaspoon chicken or mushroom bouillon powder

Dash of MSG (optional)

2 teaspoons sugar

1 large egg white

FOR THE PUFF PASTRY:

2 packages, about 2 pounds (907 g) or 4 large sheets, puff pastry (thawed if previously frozen)

FOR THE EGG WASH:

1 egg yolk

1 tablespoon (15 ml) milk or plant-based milk

1. Preheat the oven to 375°F (190°C) with a rack in the center. Line 1 or 2 large baking sheets with parchment paper and set aside.

2. Preheat a wok or frying pan over medium-high heat until it smokes. Add 1 tablespoon (15 ml) neutral oil, then sauté the minced onions until they're translucent, a few minutes. Add the garlic and cook for an additional minute. Remove from heat and let cool completely.

3. Make the filling. In a large bowl, combine the ground pork, fish sauce, oyster sauce, Shaoxing wine, soy sauce, cornstarch, black pepper, chicken or mushroom powder, optional MSG, sugar, egg white, and optional sesame paste. Mix in the cooled onion and garlic.

4. On a lightly floured surface, roll out the puff pastry to about ⅙-inch (4 mm) thickness and use a 3-inch (7 cm) biscuit or cookie cutter to cut out 48 circles. Spoon 1 to 1½ tablespoons of the filling into the center of 24 of the circles. These will be the bottoms of your pastries.

5. Make the egg wash by beating the egg yolk and milk in a small bowl.

6. Using a pastry brush, brush the edges of the filled pastry circles with egg wash and place an unfilled circle on top of each to form a lid. Press the edges to seal and use a fork to score around the edges to further seal.

7. Transfer the assembled pastries to the prepared baking sheet and brush the tops with egg wash.

8. Bake until the pastries are shiny, golden brown and puffy and your kitchen smells super delicious, about 20 to 25 minutes.

9. Remove from the oven and cool on a wire rack. Serve hot for the best taste!

10. There will be leftover filling that can be refrigerated for up to 4 days or frozen for up to 3 months. Use it to make more pâté chaud another day, or try using the filling to make dumplings!

NOTE: *A popular dim sum dish is* char siu sou *(also known as Chinese barbecue pork pie), which features a sweeter puff pastry filled with char siu. These pies are typically glazed with honey and garnished with sesame seeds. If you're interested in trying something different, you can make char siu sou by substituting the pâté chaud filling with the THW Char Siu Bao filling recipe found on page 56.*

TIP: *These pastries can be shaped into squares, but I prefer them round, because rounded pâté chaud are the ones I remember having as a child. Honestly, you can even make them heart-shaped, or any shape you desire.*

PREP TIME	30 MINUTES
COOK TIME	30 MINUTES
YIELD	ABOUT 25 PASTRIES

Dim Sum–Style Steamed Spare Ribs

I had a heated debate with myself: Should I add a steamed chicken feet or a spare ribs recipe to this book? Spare ribs emerged as the clear winner, obviously, and let's face it: Who can resist these succulent bites of meaty goodness? Don't get me wrong; I'm not suggesting that it's a competition between the two dishes. It's more of a word count issue in cookbooks, dang it (although a dim sum cook-off show would be pretty epic!). There's just something universally appealing about spare ribs. Whenever I hit up a dim sum joint, I never fail to order this dish. Sinking your teeth into the juicy, tender, flavorful meat and nibbling on cartilage—it's pure primal joy. If you want to take your spare ribs to the next level, be sure to marinate them for at least 30 minutes, or even better, overnight.

FOR THE RIBS:

1½ pounds (680 g) fatty spare ribs, cut into 1-inch (2.5-cm) or bite-size segments (you may want to ask your butcher to precut the spare ribs for you)

1 teaspoon salt

FOR THE MARINADE:

2 garlic cloves, chopped

1 teaspoon minced ginger

4 tablespoons (60 ml) soy sauce

2 tablespoons (26 g) sugar

Dash of MSG

1 teaspoon chicken or mushroom powder

2 tablespoons (30 ml) oyster sauce

1 teaspoon white pepper

4 tablespoons (60 ml) Shaoxing wine

2 tablespoons (30 ml) sesame oil

2 teaspoons Chinkiang vinegar

1 tablespoon (8.4 g) dried mandarin orange peel, rehydrated in water for a few minutes (optional)

FOR THE CORNSTARCH SLURRY:

1 tablespoon (8 g) cornstarch

2 tablespoons (30 ml) water

FOR STEAMING:

About 3.5 ounces (100 g) taro, diced (optional, but recipe tester Claire Fan highly recommends it and thinks you should add even more)

1 teaspoon salt, adjust to taste

1 teaspoon Chinese fermented black beans, washed and drained (optional but recommended)

2 red chili peppers, deseeded and chopped

¼ large green bell pepper, deseeded and diced finely (optional)

1 tablespoon (15 ml) neutral oil

¼ cup (4 g) chopped cilantro (optional)

Sesame seeds (optional)

Fire Chili Crisp Oil (page 176) (optional)

1. Lightly season the spare ribs with the salt.

2. In a large bowl, mix together all the marinade ingredients. In a separate small bowl, mix the cornstarch with water to form a slurry. Add the slurry to the marinade and mix well.

3. Add the spare ribs and taro, if using, and stir until evenly coated. Cover and refrigerate for at least 30 minutes.

4. Prepare a steamer setup according to the instructions on page 15. Transfer the marinated spare ribs to a dish or plate (or mini dim sum plates) and garnish with the optional black beans and peppers. Drizzle the oil over the spare ribs. Place the spare ribs into the steamer(s) and cover.

5. Steam over medium-high heat until the spare ribs reach an internal temperature of 145°F (63°C) and the taro has softened, about 18 to 20 minutes. Periodically check the water level and replenish with hot water as needed.

6. Remove from the steamer and top with optional cilantro or sesame seeds, if desired. Serve hot with optional chili crisp oil.

PREP TIME	20 MINUTES
COOK TIME	20 MINUTES
INACTIVE TIME	30 MINUTES OR LONGER
YIELD	4 TO 6 SERVINGS

NOTE: These spare ribs would also be a lovely substitute for my Cantonese-Style Stir-Fried Chicken Ding (page 110), over the Hong Kong Clay Pot Rice (page 124).

Tony's Spicy Cumin Lamb Skewers

At a young age, I learned you could ~~bribe~~ befriend almost anyone with food, thanks to playing video games like *Harvest Moon* and *The Sims*. (In those games, you keep gifting nonplayer characters [NPCs] presents or food until they like you. Some will even try to marry you.) Just bribe, I mean befriend, people with your home-made food! Or, in my third best guy friend's case, Tony lures friends (us) in with his amazing cumin lamb skewers.

Every time we visit Tony's house, Philip asks, "Are you making lamb sticks, Tony?" to our embarrassment and Tony's amusement. Of course, if given a chance, our nine-year-old would down a handful of these irresistible

lamb skewers in one sitting, to further embarrass us. Then Jake and I would join him.

Cumin lamb skewers originate in Xinjiang, China, toward the north and near Mongolia, where the winters are long and cold. Often seasoned with Middle Eastern spices that can pack a kick, these skewers are perfect during the wintertime, though these days, we have them in the summer at one of Tony's barbecues. They always remind me of the $2 lamb sticks I used to get from street vendors in Flushing, but honestly, they're so much better when homemade by my wonderful friend, Tony.

About 2 pounds (910 g) well-marbled lamb shoulder or lamb leg meat, cut into about ½-inch (1 cm) bite-size pieces (keep the fat)

FOR THE MARINADE:

2 teaspoons salt

1 teaspoon sugar

2 teaspoons garlic powder

2 teaspoons ground cumin

½ teaspoon white pepper

2 tablespoons (7 g) red chili flakes

2 teaspoons Sichuan peppercorns (optional)

2 teaspoons fennel seeds (optional)

2 teaspoons whole cumin seeds (optional)

2 tablespoons (30 ml) neutral or sesame oil

4 tablespoons (60 ml) Shaoxing wine

3 tablespoons (45 ml) soy sauce

1½ teaspoons rice or black vinegar

1. Make the marinade. If you have a mortar and pestle or a spice grinder, coarsely and briefly grind the salt, sugar, garlic powder, cumin, white pepper, chili flakes, and the optional peppercorn, fennel seeds, and cumin seeds together. Regardless of whether or not you ground the spices, add them to a bowl or container large enough to marinate the lamb. Remove about 1 tablespoon of this spice mixture and set aside. Then add the oil, wine, soy sauce, and vinegar and mix to the larger portion of spice mixture to make a marinade.

2. Add the lamb and stir well. Massage and rub the marinade into the lamb with your hands. Cover and refrigerate for up to 60 minutes.

3. Thread the lamb onto the skewers, lengthwise, and pack them closely together. If your lamb pieces are small, thread about 10 pieces to a skewer, leaving at least 3 inches (7 cm) left of a handle on the bottom. The skewer's pointy tip should be exposed at the top. Repeat until you have about 10 to 12 lamb skewers.

4. Cook the lamb skewers. While you can broil the skewers in the oven, they are most delicious when cooked over a grill. Once the charcoal in your grill has gray ash, set the skewers down on the oiled grilling grate and cook for 2 minutes. Flip and cook for another 2 minutes. Carefully sprinkle the reserved spice mixture over all sides of the lamb, and cook until all sides are seared, a few minutes. You may have to flip the skewers a few times. I have never seen street vendors or Tony covering the grill when cooking lamb skewers, so I advise cooking them uncovered.

5. Remove the lamb skewers from the grill and serve immediately, smoking-hot delicious. No sauce is needed, though if you have any spice mixture left, feel free to sprinkle more onto the lamb skewers as needed.

NOTE: *Please have 10 to 12 bamboo skewers handy. It's best to soak bamboo skewers in water for 30 minutes to 2 hours before grilling. The wetness prevents the bamboo skewers from burning quickly over a hot grill.*

TIP: *These skewers can also be cooked with an indoor electric grill or a tabletop grill.*

PREP TIME	25 MINUTES
COOK TIME	ABOUT 20 TO 30 MINUTES
YIELD	10 TO 12 SKEWERS

Chinatown
Jammy
Tea Eggs

Before going down the stairs of Grand Street station to head back to Coney Island, my mother would always buy us treats from Chinatown street vendors. My sister and I loved the tea leaf eggs, especially. Those marinated eggs were salty, full of umami, and a messy delight to peel, revealing their beautiful secrets. The egg white is brown-webbed and marbled with tea and soy sauce. Just one egg was a tease, but even having two each wasn't enough.

Though my mom knew how to make these eggs at home (you'll see it's a relatively simple recipe), she made it a point to support Chinatown street vendors and give them our business, even though we also struggled financially. It's always the people who have the least to give who give their all, no?

Originating from the Zhejiang Province of China, these eggs are traditionally hard-boiled. Since I love melt-in-your-mouth jammy eggs, we're going to give this dish a modern spin using soft-boiled eggs. I've also tried using different tea, like barley tea, and experimentation pays off!

6 large eggs

FOR THE MARINADE:

2 tablespoons (30 ml) soy sauce

3 tablespoons (45 ml) dark soy sauce

3 cups (705 ml) water

3 bay leaves

1½ tablespoons (20 g) brown sugar

1½ teaspoons salt

1 cinnamon stick

3 star anises

2 tablespoons (12 g) black tea leaves, any brand (or choose another type of tea!)

1 teaspoon Sichuan peppercorns or chili flakes (optional)

1 tablespoon (10 g) minced garlic, shallots, or scallions (optional but recommended)

1 teaspoon sesame oil (optional)

1 teaspoon sesame seeds (optional)

Dash of MSG (optional)

MAKE IT VEGAN:
Use this vegan marinade to marinate seitan, mushrooms, tofu, or other plant-based proteins.

1. Combine all marinade ingredients in a heavy saucepan. Cook over medium-high heat until boiling, then reduce the heat to low and simmer for 6 to 10 minutes. Remove from heat and allow to cool.

2. Soft-boil the eggs. In a large saucepan, bring enough water to submerge the eggs to a rolling boil. Carefully add the eggs using a ladle or slotted spoon, then reduce the heat to medium-low for a gentle simmer. Cook, covered, for 6 minutes to achieve soft-boiled eggs with jammy, runny yolks. (For medium-boiled eggs, cook for 7 to 8 minutes; for hard-boiled eggs, cook for 10 minutes or longer.)

3. While the eggs cook, prepare a bowl of ice water.

4. Transfer the eggs to the ice water using a slotted spoon, and let them sit for about 5 minutes. This will cool the eggs and prevent further cooking.

5. To create a marbled appearance, use the back of a spoon to tap the eggshells, forming both large cracks and hairline fractures. Alternatively, peel off the entire shell for a more uniform brown color and enhanced flavor. Repeat with the remaining eggs.

6. Place the eggs in an airtight container or silicone food storage bag, and strain in the marinade. (Alternatively, transfer the eggs directly to the saucepan with the marinade and cover.) Refrigerate overnight or for at least 12 hours.

7. Remove the eggs from the container, peel as needed, and enjoy. Traditionally, tea eggs are boiled in the marinade, and the color is deeper. When the eggs are just soaked, the trade-off for the jamminess is a lighter webbing shade. It'll still be delicious though, and feel free to dip the eggs in the marinade before eating and lick your fingers!

NOTE: You won't be able to enjoy these eggs immediately, as you'll be marinating them for at least 12 hours or overnight. For the impatient, you can simmer the eggs in the marinade over low heat for about 30 minutes and then enjoy them hot or warm, but the yolks will no longer be runny and jammy. Also, there's enough marinade for more than 6 eggs, and you can always freeze the marinade, store it, and reboil it for the next batch of eggs.

TIP: Adding a splash of white vinegar and a teaspoon of salt to the boiling water before adding the eggs may help prevent the eggs from cracking, and they'll be easier to peel once cooled. People also swear by pricking a small hole into one of the tips of the eggs to prevent them from cracking. Jake does this when he uses his egg steamer. I'm too lazy and always skip the hole-pricking step.

PREP TIME	10 MINUTES
COOK TIME	20 MINUTES
INACTIVE TIME	APPROXIMATELY 12 HOURS
YIELD	6 EGGS

Taiwanese Popcorn Chicken from Flushing

I can't recall if I was eleven or twelve years old when I first tasted Taiwanese popcorn chicken in an underground food court in Flushing, New York. It's funny how I also can't remember what I wore that day, or whether it was winter or summer. There's one detail I'll never forget though: how enjoyable it was to eat Taiwanese popcorn chicken for the first time, spearing each piece of perfectly crispy and juicy fried chicken with a toothpick, popping it into my mouth, and relishing the hot burst of flavor. The fried basil accompanying the chicken was equally delicious. If you're seeking a deeply satisfying snack or appetizer, look no further; this gluten-free fried chicken is sure to please! Oh, and if you can find soft chicken knee bones, try mixing them in with the chicken meat.

FOR THE MARINADE:

2½ tablespoons (38 ml) soy sauce

1 tablespoon (15 ml) Shaoxing wine

1 teaspoon sesame oil

1 teaspoon five-spice powder

1 teaspoon ground white pepper

1 teaspoon granulated sugar

1 teaspoon garlic powder

2 teaspoons cornstarch

1 teaspoon rice vinegar

FOR SPRINKLING MIXTURE (OPTIONAL):

1 teaspoon salt

1 teaspoon sugar

2 teaspoons Sichuan or black peppercorns (optional)

Paprika (optional)

Chili powder (optional)

Dash of cumin or pinch of cumin seeds

Sesame seeds

FOR FRYING:

1 pound (454 g) skinless chicken thigh, cut into bite-size pieces and seasoned with salt and pepper, adjust to taste

1 cup (128 g) tapioca starch or potato starch

1 cup (40 g) Thai or sweet basil, washed and dried

1. Create the marinade by combining all marinade ingredients in a large bowl or airtight container. Add the chicken and mix thoroughly, using your hands as needed to massage the marinade into the chicken. Cover and refrigerate for at least 30 minutes or up to overnight.

2. If desired, create the optional sprinkling mixture by grinding the ingredients using a mortar and pestle. Set aside.

3. Coat and "seed" the chicken. Place the tapioca starch or potato starch in a shallow bowl and mix. Add the chicken, wet your hands, and toss the chicken to ensure even coating with the tapioca starch. The chicken is ready for frying when small beads or seeds of tapioca batter form on its surface. You may need to wet your hands again during this process.

4. Fry the chicken. Heat enough neutral oil to submerge the chicken in a pot or deep fryer to 350°F (180°C). Carefully add the chicken in small batches and fry until golden brown and crispy all over, a few minutes.

5. Remove the chicken from the oil using a kitchen spider or slotted spoon and drain on a paper towel–lined plate or wire rack.

6. Flash-fry the dried basil leaves until they become crispy, shiny, and translucent, about 30 seconds or less. Garnish the chicken with the fried basil, and sprinkle with the optional spice mixture. While they're amazing without sauce, I love dipping this chicken in ketchup or Fiery Hot Mayo (page 174).

TIP: *For added flavor, crush up your favorite potato chips like Doritos or Cheetos and mix that into your potato or tapioca starch before coating the chicken.*

PREP TIME	**25 MINUTES**
COOK TIME	**ABOUT 30 MINUTES**
INACTIVE TIME	**30 MINUTES TO OVERNIGHT**
YIELD	**4 TO 6 SERVINGS**

MAKE IT VEGAN: Firm tofu or diced portobello mushroom would be great alternatives. If you don't have Thai basil handy, you can fry some chopped kale or garnish with chopped scallions instead.

Air-Fried Sesame Shrimp Toast with Bang Bang Sauce

Mom said, "很脆 (very crispy)," as she took another bite of the air-fried sesame shrimp toast I had just prepared for lunch. "Just like the ones back in Hong Kong," she added while crunching away and giving me a thumbs-up, as if she could read my mind. It's amusing (and somewhat melancholy) that, even at nearly 40, I still crave her approval.

Anyway, shrimp toast is ideal when made with milk bread, and you should mince the shrimp vigorously to achieve a pastelike consistency. Take your anger out on that shrimp, okay? After marinating for a few minutes, air-fry or convection bake the toast, and each bite will be flavorful, delicate, and crispy. Drizzle with fresh lemon juice, as acidity pairs well with seafood (and anything savory, really), and dip the toast into bang bang sauce or spicy mayo. Take a bite, and fall in love. I bet you'll want to make this dish repeatedly as a party finger food, appetizer, for brunch, or even in your dreams, LOL.

About 10 ounces (283 g) shrimp, washed, peeled, and deveined

FOR THE MARINADE:

1 egg white

Dash of MSG (optional)

1 tablespoon (8 g) cornstarch

¼ teaspoon white pepper

1 teaspoon Shaoxing wine

½ to 1 teaspoon sesame oil

1 teaspoon soy sauce

Pinch of granulated sugar

FOR THE TOAST:

4 slices of milk bread (white bread is okay too), with all the crust removed

Black or white sesame seeds

2 teaspoons panko bread crumbs

1 large egg, beaten, for egg wash

Cooking spray or a few slices of unsalted butter

A few lemon wedges (optional)

FOR THE OPTIONAL BANG BANG SAUCE:

⅓ cup (75 g) mayonnaise

1½ tablespoons (22 ml) sriracha or 1 teaspoon gochujang, adjust to taste

2 tablespoons (30 ml) sweet Thai chili sauce, adjust to taste

2 teaspoons honey or agave nectar, adjust to taste

Pinch of MSG

1. Finely mince the shrimp until it reaches a paste-like consistency, then transfer it to a bowl or food storage container. Add all the marinade ingredients and mix thoroughly until the mixture becomes cohesive and sticky. Let the shrimp marinate for about 10 minutes, or cover and refrigerate overnight for later use if desired.

2. Line a baking sheet with parchment paper and preheat the oven to 400°F (200°C) on convection mode if available. If using an air fryer, skip this step.

3. Divide the shrimp mixture into 4 equal portions, and spread each portion evenly over a slice of bread. Top with sesame seeds and panko. Brush the tops with egg wash, and spray with cooking spray or add slices of butter.

4. If using an oven, place the bread on the prepared baking sheet and bake for 5 minutes. Then, reduce the temperature to 350°F (180°C) and continue baking until the toast is golden brown and the shrimp is cooked through, for another 5 minutes. If using an air fryer, air-fry at 400°F (200°C) for 5 minutes, then lower the temperature to 350°F (180°C) and air-fry for an additional 5 minutes.

5. While the shrimp toast is cooking, if desired, make the optional bang bang sauce by combining all the sauce ingredients in a bowl. Set aside.

6. Once the shrimp toast is ready, remove it from the oven or air fryer and cut into triangular wedges or rectangles. Squeeze a little lemon juice over the top and dip into the optional sauce, if you made it. Fiery Hot Mayo (page 174) and *Fire* Chili Crisp Oil (page 176) also go well with this fun finger food. Enjoy!

TIP: *For an added crunch, add about 1 tablespoon diced Japanese mountain yam or water chestnut to the shrimp mixture.*

NOTE: You can use Fiery Hot Mayo (page 174) instead of bang bang sauce.

PREP TIME	10 MINUTES
COOK TIME	10 TO 15 MINUTES
YIELD	2 TO 4 SERVINGS

ONE-PAN WONDERS

"Cooking is like love. It should be entered into with abandon, or not at all."
—*Julia Child*

One day, feeling particularly adventurous (my code word for masochistic), I decided to host a dinner party for more than 15 people, where I would prepare... everything. That whirlwind of a Saturday found me cooking and roasting various dishes in just a few hours, creating eight delectable one-pan/one-sheet meals. Among these were my usual crowd-pleasers: the irresistibly Juicy and Crispy Baked "Fried" Chicken (page 88) and my Savory and Sweet Soy Salmon (page 99). Since then, my motto has been to work smarter, not harder, enabling me to make scrumptious meals using just a frying pan or baking sheet. Some of these meals include my neighbor Mary Usha's Tandoori Chicken and Raita (page 80), and my dad's Saucy Egg, Beef, and Gai Lan Stir-Fry (page 94)—a dish he created out of love for his daughters.

I cook for my family of four almost daily and often rely on the recipes found in this chapter, especially when time is limited. Or when I'm feeling a bit lazy or experiencing high-functioning depression. There are days when the sun in Seattle might be shining outside, but inside of me, there's a relentless cloud that refuses to shift. High-functioning depression isn't visible like a broken ankle, but it's just as real, just as painful. It's just different. And yet the world doesn't stop, and neither do the hungry mouths to feed.

For those days, I've perfected these recipes. Simple, yet nourishing. Here's to feeding our bodies and, little by little, our souls.

My apologies if that was a little deep. Maybe I should have added a trigger warning: #mentalhealthmatters.

Moving on, as this chapter is protein-heavy, I recommend adding a vegetable dish from the Garden Party chapter to create a balanced dinner. Oh, and of course, once again rice pairs well with almost anything here.

MAKE IT VEGAN: Use plant-based yogurt and substitute the chicken with plant-based protein. For the raita, use vegan yogurt and omit the honey or substitute it with maple syrup.

Mary Usha's Tandoori Chicken and Raita

My neighbor and beloved friend Mary Usha served my family and me this unforgettable dish at our first dinner party. That night, I asked for seconds (and thirds). The chicken was succulent, flavorful, and so darn juicy, thanks to a yogurt-based marinade infused with garam masala, cumin, and coriander.

Mary Usha served this dish with both rice and homemade naan, mint chutney, and her versatile and refreshing raita, an Indian condiment. Her chil-

dren, Yashika and Karthik, are lucky, and I've asked her to adopt me on multiple occasions now that both kids are away at college! Mary Usha (to my mother's delight) has yet to adopt me, alas, but she did share her recipe here! This is a perfect one-pan dish for a busy weeknight dinner; just be sure to marinate the chicken the night before.

RECIPE SPECS

FOR THE WET RUB:

1 teaspoon paprika

½ teaspoon cayenne or chili powder

1 tablespoon (15 ml) lemon juice

FOR THE CHICKEN:

1 pound (454 g) skinless chicken drumsticks or thighs

1 large red or white onion, sliced (reserve some for garnishing)

A few lemon wedges

FOR THE MARINADE:

½ cup (115 g) plain yogurt or plain Greek yogurt

1 tablespoon (14 g) garam masala (Indian spice blend, store-bought)

1½ teaspoons minced ginger

1 tablespoon (10 g) minced garlic (or ½ teaspoon garlic powder)

1 teaspoon salt

1 teaspoon ground cumin

1 teaspoon ground coriander

2 tablespoons (30 ml) lemon juice, adjust to taste

A few drops red food coloring gel (optional)

FOR THE OPTIONAL RAITA:

1 cup (230 g) plain full-fat yogurt or Greek yogurt

1 teaspoon cumin powder, chaat masala, or garam masala

Salt and black pepper to taste

1 teaspoon honey or granulated sugar

Squirt of fresh lime juice (optional)

½ cucumber, peeled and diced

¼ cup (4 g) chopped fresh cilantro

¼ cup (4 g) chopped fresh mint (optional)

1 chopped hot chili (Thai, serrano, Indian, bird's eye) (optional)

FOR GARNISHING (OPTIONAL):

Chopped parsley or cilantro

Sliced raw onions

PREP TIME	20 MINUTES
COOK TIME	40 MINUTES
INACTIVE TIME	4 HOURS TO OVERNIGHT
YIELD	4 TO 6 SERVINGS

1. Mix the wet rub ingredients together in a medium bowl. Place the chicken in a shallow dish or storage container and season with salt. Massage the wet rub all over the chicken.

2. Prepare the marinade in the same medium bowl by combining the yogurt, garam masala, ginger, garlic, salt, cumin, and coriander. If using, gradually add drops of red food coloring gel and mix until the marinade turns a light reddish color. Note that the color will deepen as the chicken cooks.

3. Pour the marinade over the chicken and rub it in, ensuring an even coating on all sides. Cover the dish and refrigerate for at least 4 hours or overnight.

4. Preheat the oven to 425°F (220°C). Line a baking sheet with greased parchment paper or greased aluminum foil.

5. Transfer the chicken to the prepared baking sheet. Scatter the sliced onions over the chicken. Bake until the internal temperature reaches 165°F to 170°F (75° to 76°C), about 40 minutes. Alternatively, air-fry the chicken for about 20 minutes at 400°F (200°C).

6. Allow the chicken to rest for a few minutes. Meanwhile, prepare the *raita*. Combine the yogurt, spices, salt, pepper, honey or sugar, and optional lime juice. Gently fold in the cucumbers and herbs. Top with the optional chili if using.

7. Garnish the chicken with optional parsley or cilantro and fresh lemon juice. Enjoy with the raita, naan, or basmati rice. Adding raw onions on top of the chicken adds an extra layer of flavor, as Mary Usha and her family love to do, and luckily, you have some reserved for this.

NOTE: *Chicken wings and boneless chicken breast can also be used; just adjust the cooking time so as not to overcook the different cuts of chicken. Wings take about 25 minutes to bake; chicken breast, depending on the thickness of the fillet, about 20 minutes.*

Mary Usha holding her homemade chicken biryani, 2023

Mouthwatering Tonkatsu

Whenever I'm in Japan, I never pass up the opportunity to dig into some tasty katsu dishes. Whether it's *katsu don* (a fried cutlet with egg, sauce, and rice), *tonkatsu karē* (a fried pork cutlet with curry), or *katsu sando* (cutlet sandwich), I enjoy them all. When I'm back home in my own kitchen, I love serving up tonkatsu with either Tonkatsu Sauce (page 172) or a side of Japanese curry.

This recipe is all about simplicity and great flavor. Start by seasoning the cutlets, then coat them in panko bread crumbs. You've got options for cooking your katsu: shallow frying, air-frying, deep-frying, or baking. Whichever method you choose, you'll end up with a delicious crowd-pleaser that's equally well-suited to rushed weeknights or leisurely weekends.

4 thinly sliced pork cutlets (boneless loin chops, about 1-inch [2.5 cm] thick each)

Salt and pepper, to taste

½ to 1 cup (48 to 96 g) all-purpose flour

2 eggs, beaten

1 to 2 cups (115 to 230 g) panko bread crumbs

Neutral oil, for frying

¼ to ½ head of cabbage, shredded or sliced thinly (optional but recommended)

Tonkatsu Sauce (optional but recommended, see page 172)

Black or white sesame seeds (optional)

1. Tenderize the pork cutlets using a mallet, the back of a cleaver, or a rolling pin. Season with salt and pepper. Be generous with the seasoning for thicker cutlets.

2. Set up your breading station by placing the flour, eggs, and bread crumbs in separate shallow bowls.

3. First, dredge the cutlets in the flour, shaking off any excess. Then, dip in the eggs, allowing any excess to drip off. Finally, coat with the bread crumbs, pressing gently to ensure adherence.

4. Heat about 1 inch (2.5 cm) neutral oil in a large heavy-bottomed pan over medium-high heat until it reaches 340°F (170°C).

5. Lower the heat to medium and add the pork to the hot oil. Cook until golden brown and cooked through, a few minutes per side. Rest the cutlets and then perform a second frying for 30 seconds on each side, until thoroughly crispy and golden brown.

6. Transfer the pork to a plate lined with paper towels to absorb any excess oil.

7. Serve immediately with the optional tonkatsu sauce, shredded cabbage, and steamed white rice. Optionally, sprinkle sesame seeds over the sauce and cabbage.

8. If you'd like to try a tonkatsu sandwich, place the tonkatsu on a slice of milk bread, spread with tonkatsu sauce, and top with shredded cabbage, sesame seeds, and another slice of milk bread.

TIPS: To make this gluten-free, use gluten-free panko bread crumbs and 1-1 gluten-free flour. To bake the tonkatsu, drizzle neutral oil on the breaded cutlets and bake at 400°F (200°C) on a parchment paper– or aluminum-lined baking sheet until the pork reaches an internal temperature of 145°F (63°C), about 18 minutes. Broil for an additional 1 to 2 minutes, until golden brown.

MAKE IT VEGAN: Replace the pork with firm tofu slices or eggplant or portobello mushroom slices, and substitute eggs with a vegan egg replacer. Note that Kikkoman's panko is vegan.

PREP TIME	20 MINUTES
COOK TIME	APPROXIMATELY 20 MINUTES
YIELD	4 SERVINGS

Sexy Sizzling Sisig

Jake introduced me to Filipino food at Max's Restaurant in Jersey City. He ordered a sizzling *sisig* plate, which instantly became one of my favorite dishes ever. I love squirting fresh lemon juice (use calamansi if you have it handy) on the pork as it sizzles on the hot plate. The more acidity, the better for me since "sisig" in Kapampangan means "to snack on something sour."

Sisig is buttery and tangy, irresistibly crave-worthy and satisfying. I knew I had to re-create this dish at home. It's important to note that there are several

ways to make sisig. Jake told me he has always enjoyed sisig with diced pig's ear, a specialty in Bacolod City, where he grew up. Sisig often also includes chicken liver, mayonnaise, or even pig snout or ears. After tasting different variations of sisig, I always return to the version I first fell in love with, similar to what I had the first time at Max's Restaurant and now at Max's of Manila in Tukwila, Washington.

Let me know what you think of my sisig recipe here. I hope you find it as sexy as its name.

FOR THE PORK BELLY:

1½ pounds (680 g) pork belly, skin on

Salt and pepper, to taste

1 teaspoon five-spice powder, adjust to taste

1 teaspoon garlic powder

FOR THE SAUCE:

4 tablespoons (60 ml) soy sauce

1 teaspoon Maggi or liquid aminos

1 tablespoon (15 ml) lemon or calamansi juice

¼ teaspoon black pepper

3 bay leaves

2 chili peppers, finely chopped, or ½ teaspoon chili flakes (optional)

1 teaspoon black vinegar

1 teaspoon sugar, adjust to taste

FOR THE SISIG:

1 big onion, red or white, finely chopped

4 garlic cloves, chopped

1-inch (2.5 cm) ginger, minced (optional)

¼ cup (56 g) unsalted butter

2 large eggs (optional)

3 scallions, chopped

Kewpie or mayonnaise in a squeezable container (optional)

A few lemon, lime, or calamansi wedges

1. Preheat the oven to 400°F (205°C) with a rack in the center. Line a baking sheet with aluminum foil.

2. Fill a pot with enough water to submerge the pork. Bring to a rolling boil, add a teaspoon of salt and the pork belly (skin side down). Simmer on medium-low heat for 5 minutes, then remove and set aside. Once cool, season the pork with salt, pepper, five-spice powder, and garlic powder.

3. Roast the pork, skin side up, for 20 minutes. Lower the oven temperature to 350°F (180°C) and roast for an additional 10 to 15 minutes, until the skin begins to crisp. Remove from the oven and cool before chopping into bite-size pieces.

4. Combine the sauce ingredients in a bowl.

5. Preheat a wide pan, wok, or skillet over medium-high heat until it begins to smoke. Add a tablespoon of neutral oil, followed by the onion, garlic, and optional ginger. Cook until the onion is translucent, a few minutes.

6. Add the butter, and once melted, add the pork belly. Increase the heat to high and stir as you fry. Aim for the pork to become crackling and crispy, about 2 minutes.

7. Stir in the sauce. If using, add the eggs and allow them to sizzle in the butter and oil. Don't overcook as the yolks should be runny.

8. Stir in half of the scallions, then transfer the sisig to a serving plate. Drizzle with mayonnaise and top with the rest of the scallions. Serve hot with citrus wedges on the side and white or Filipino garlic rice (*sinangag*).

NOTE: *Sisig is often served on a sizzling plate. If you have a sizzling plate and know how to use it carefully and safely at home, transfer the cooked dish to a prepared sizzling plate and serve. It will involve heating the plate in the oven.*

MAKE IT VEGAN: Replace the pork with firm tofu, seitan, or a vegan alternative protein. Omit the eggs and use vegan butter and vegan mayo.

PREP TIME	**30 MINUTES**
COOK TIME	**50 TO 60 MINUTES**
YIELD	**4 SERVINGS**

Savory Green Onion and Kimchi Korean Pancakes

Typically served as appetizers, Korean pancakes such as *haemul pajeon* (해물파전, seafood pancakes) and *kimchijeon* (김치전, kimchi pancakes) are popular features in Korean restaurants in America. My family loves ordering Korean pancakes, so I just had to develop this recipe so we can always enjoy these at home. Loaded with scallions, kimchi, and your preferred protein if desired (I love oysters and shrimp), these pancakes are crispy on the outside with a slightly chewy texture from the tapioca starch. They make an irresistible

starter, especially for those who love a spicy kick! We won't hold back on the kimchi; use at least half a cup, or more if you prefer. We'll also be generous with the scallions, incorporating them abundantly into this kimchi-pajeon or kimchijeon.

This recipe yields two medium-size (5- to 6-inch or 12- to 15-cm) pancakes for ease of flipping. If you're bold enough to attempt a large (9- to 10-inch or 22- to 25-cm) pancake, you'll need two spatulas and some finesse.

FOR THE OPTIONAL DIPPING SAUCE:

1 recipe Kat's Everyday Dipping Sauce (page 166)

FOR THE PANCAKES:

2 tablespoons (30 ml) kimchi juice (from the jar, but water works too)

1 cup (125 g) all-purpose flour

1 cup (235 ml) cold water or vegetable broth

2 tablespoons (20 g) tapioca starch (adds a slight chew)

Some chili flakes or 1 teaspoon gochujang for extra spice

Dash of garlic powder (optional)

1 teaspoon chicken or mushroom bouillon powder

1 teaspoon miso or doenjang

½ teaspoon salt

¼ teaspoon white pepper or a dash of black pepper

½ cup (105 g) kimchi, chopped and patted dry with paper towels, divided into 2 even portions (add more kimchi if you'd like)

About 10 scallions, washed, dried, and chopped into thirds (about 4-inch [10-cm] long segments), divided into 2 even portions

FOR GREASING THE PAN:

2 tablespoons (30 ml) neutral oil, more as needed

FOR TOPPING THE PANCAKE, OPTIONAL:

Black or white sesame seeds

Scallions, chopped

Fried shallots or onions

1. Make optional dipping sauce if desired, then set aside.

2. Make the pancake batter. Combine all pancake ingredients (except for the kimchi and scallions) in a large bowl to form a smooth batter. Add kimchi and scallions to the batter and ensure they're evenly covered.

3. Make the pancakes. Preheat a skillet or pan over medium heat. Add the oil, then carefully ladle in half the batter, shaping it with a spatula into a circle about ¼ inch (6 mm) in thickness. Cook for 2 to 4 minutes until the edges appear golden brown and crispy. Adjust the heat as needed.

4. When the pancake edges are crackling, crispy, and golden brown, carefully flip the pancake and continue to cook until the other side is also golden brown and crispy, approximately 3 to 4 minutes. Flip once more and cook for another 2 to 3 minutes to ensure the batter is cooked through. If unsure, reduce the heat to medium-low, cover the pan, and cook for an additional minute.

5. Remove from heat and place on paper towels to absorb any excess oil. Repeat steps 3 to 5 for the second pancake.

6. Slice each pancake into 6 to 8 pieces, garnish with optional toppings, and serve with the optional dipping sauce.

TIP: *Add ⅓ cup cooked protein (chopped Spam, ham, firm tofu, mushrooms, shrimp, or other seafood; weight varies) fried along with the kimchi and scallions before adding the pancake batter. A beaten egg can also be added to your pancake as it fries.*

MAKE IT VEGAN: Typically, kimchi is not vegan as it's made with fish sauce or shrimp paste. To make this dish vegan, you can find vegan kimchi in supermarkets. Use mushroom powder and plant-based proteins, if adding any.

PREP TIME	10 MINUTES
COOK TIME	10 MINUTES
YIELD	4 SERVINGS

Super Juicy and Crispy Baked "Fried" Chicken

If this is the second one of my cookbooks you've picked up, then you'd know that I rarely baked growing up because the oven in my childhood home was always stuffed with pots and pans. (I've learned over the years that this is very common in many Asian diaspora households, LOL!) This recipe is a cherished exception. On the rare occasion when we did bake, Mom and I would roast the crispiest and juiciest chicken in the oven. It could even pass as fried chicken! Fried chicken zealots might disagree, but that's okay, as this

recipe is deeply satisfying for someone like me who has never enjoyed deep-frying food at home. This dish also fed my family through the years, from the nineties in Coney Island, to the present day in Seattle.

In a pinch, I would use my favorite seasoning mix (Seasons Spicy Bake Mix), but if you can't find that at your local Asian supermarket or online, use the spices I've listed in the ingredients list.

GLUTEN-FREE

RECIPE SPECS

2 scallions, cut into 4-inch (10-cm) segments

6 garlic cloves

1 whole chicken, halved

Salt and pepper, to taste

Chicken or mushroom bouillon powder

Garlic powder

Five-spice powder (optional)

Baking powder for dusting

Potato starch for dusting

Olive, canola, or other neutral oil for drizzling

Fire Chili Crisp Oil (optional, page 176) for serving

1. Preheat the oven to 475°F (240°C) with a rack in the center.

2. Line a large baking sheet with aluminum foil and spray with pan spray or brush over with oil. Place the scallions and garlic on the middle of the sheet—the chicken will rest on top of them.

3. Pat the chicken dry with paper towels. Season with salt, pepper, bouillon powder, garlic powder, and optional five-spice powder, all over. A good rule of thumb is to spread a light, even layer of each seasoning ingredient all over the chicken. Rub the seasoning into the chicken with clean or gloved hands.

4. Place the chicken, drumsticks up, on the baking sheet. Dust the skin with a light sprinkling of baking powder and potato starch. Drizzle the chicken with oil all over.

5. Roast until the chicken is cooked through, browned, and crispy, about 37 minutes. (If you have an instant-read thermometer, insert it into the thickest part of the chicken thigh, and the reading should register 165°F or 74°C.)

6. Remove from the oven. Transfer the chicken to a cutting board and let rest for about 10 minutes.

7. Cut the chicken. Using a sharp, sturdy knife, carefully slice along the leg to separate the breast and thigh. You may notice a bit of juice squirt out—yum! Next, take the breast and cut it in half, crosswise through the bone, keeping the wing intact. Then, slice through the joint connecting the drumstick to the thigh. Repeat these steps on the other half of the chicken.

8. Divide the carved chicken between 4 to 6 dishes and enjoy with steamed white rice, veggies, or salad. Drizzle with *Fire* Chili Crisp Oil if desired.

NOTE: *If this is your first cookbook by me, please do check out* Modern Asian Baking at Home, *my debut cookbook all about "baking the Asian way." Hint, hint, hint. Did you know I'm known for being not subtle at all? It's quite ironic, being the founder of a group called Subtle Asian Baking.* ☺

PREP TIME	15 MINUTES
COOK TIME	37 MINUTES
YIELD	1 WHOLE ROASTED CHICKEN

Sweet and Soy Salmon

Shortly after moving from Brooklyn to Seattle, I began hosting parties for our new friends around the neighborhood. What better way to build bonds than to feed others, right?

In a span of about four hours, I'd make enough food to feed more than fifteen people. What was my trick? Well, I relied heavily on mise en place, for one, my oven, and my one-sheet or one-pan recipes, like this one, a buttery and flaky sweet soy salmon baked to per-

fection. The marinade reminds me of teriyaki, but I use honey here instead of mixing soy sauce with mirin and sugar.

This is one of Philip's favorite dishes. Not a surprise since he loves salmon anything, especially sushi. I always make sure the inside of the salmon appears slightly undone so it's buttery and melt-in-your-mouth perfect, pleasing my little sushi lover. (You don't want to overbake salmon, because it becomes dry and papery.)

RECIPE SPECS

FOR THE MARINADE:

2 tablespoons (30 ml) soy sauce

1 teaspoon dark soy sauce

1 tablespoon (20 g) honey (adjust to taste)

2 teaspoons lemon or yuzu juice

2 teaspoons sake, rice wine, or Shaoxing wine

Salt and white pepper to taste

1 teaspoon sesame oil (optional)

1 teaspoon furu (optional)

Dash of MSG

FOR THE FISH:

1 pound (454 g) skin-on salmon fillet (the fattier, the better)

Black or white sesame seeds (optional)

3 garlic cloves, minced

2 scallions, cut into 3-inch (7.5 cm) segments

1 tablespoon (14 g) unsalted butter

1. Make the marinade by mixing all the marinade ingredients. Taste the sauce and adjust the flavor as needed.

2. Line a baking sheet with aluminum foil. Spray with pan spray or brush with neutral oil. Lay the scallions in the middle on the baking sheet. Place the salmon, skin side down, on the scallions.

3. Score the salmon by cutting shallow slits into the top. Spoon the marinade onto the fish, making sure it seeps into the slits. Add the minced garlic and optional black sesame seeds. Cover with aluminum foil and let it marinade in a cool space or the refrigerator for at least 30 minutes.

4. Preheat the oven to 350°F (180°C) with a rack in the center.

5. Remove the foil and place the butter on top of the fish. Alternatively, drizzle with olive, avocado, or any neutral oil. Bake until the middle appears slightly undone (moist, vibrantly coral, and semi-translucent), with an internal temperature of 145°F (60°C), about 15 to 17 minutes. Avoid overcooking your salmon.

6. Remove from the oven and serve immediately. This dish pairs well with warm rice, plain or buttered pasta, udon, or even a bed of salad.

TIP: If you want to try a different sauce, substitute the 2 types of soy sauce with about 1 tablespoon miso (red or white) and dilute the sauce with a little water. I suggest tasting and adjusting the sauce as you go to suit your palate.

PREP TIME	**10 MINUTES**
COOK TIME	**20 MINUTES**
INACTIVE TIME	**30 MINUTES**
YIELD	**4 SERVINGS**

Easy-Peasy
Sushi Bake

Here's an easy-peasy dish that comes with few rules and endless possibilities. Don't see corn on the ingredients list? Feel free to add it. Love shredded carrots? Include them! Fancy shrimp or scallops? Swap them in for the salmon and crabmeat, or better yet, use them all! Want to substitute mayo with softened cream cheese? Go ahead! Customize your sushi bake with your favorite veggies and seafood. This dish is a fun group activity with friends or kids and perfect for potlucks, tailgating, or as a savory afternoon snack on tranquil Sundays. It's also a favorite of mine for its simplicity and satisfaction, while still reminding one of sushi. All you need is a 9 x 9-inch (22 x 22 cm) baking dish and cooked rice ready (see instructions on page 24 for cooking rice).

FOR THE SAUCE:

2 tablespoons (30 ml) soy sauce

⅓ cup (75 g) Japanese mayo (like Kewpie)

1 tablespoon (15 ml) oyster sauce (optional)

1 tablespoon (15 ml) lemon or yuzu juice

1 tablespoon (15 ml) sesame oil

1 tablespoon (20 g) honey or agave syrup

1 tablespoon (15 ml) sriracha, gochujang (for a spicier sushi bake), or sweet chili sauce

FOR THE SUSHI BAKE:

About 1 pound (454 g) fresh salmon, cubed

½ pound (226 g) imitation crabmeat, diced

½ white or yellow onion, diced

2 tablespoons (30 ml) rice vinegar

2 tablespoons (30 ml) mirin

4 cups (600 g) cooked sushi rice or short-grain rice

Roasted nori (or seaweed) pieces

FOR THE OPTIONAL TOPPINGS:

Furikake or sesame seeds

Unagi (eel) sauce or Japanese sushi sauce

Sliced avocados (recommended)

Chopped scallions

Wakame salad (or Japanese seaweed salad)

1. Make the sauce by mixing all the sauce ingredients in a large bowl. Mix in the salmon, crabmeat, and onion. Set aside.

2. Drizzle the rice vinegar and mirin over the rice and fluff to combine.

3. Assemble the sushi bake. Spread a layer of rice evenly in the bottom of a 9 x 9-inch (23 x 23-cm) baking dish. Then layer the salmon and crabmeat mixture evenly on top of the rice.

4. Place a rack at the top and broil the sushi bake on high, until the tops are slightly charred, about 5 to 10 minutes.

5. Remove from the oven and add optional toppings, like a layer of sliced avocado. Drizzle with *unagi* (eel) sauce and additional mayo. Sprinkle with scallions and furikake or sesame seeds.

6. Serve by scooping a generous portion from all layers of the sushi bake onto a piece of seaweed. Fold the seaweed over the sushi bake and pop it straight into your mouth.

NOTE: Rather than broiling, you can bake the dish at 350°F (180°C) for about 15 minutes. Anything over 18 minutes may overcook the salmon.

TIP: If you buy sushi-grade salmon, you can enjoy this dish without baking the salmon (but please do bake cold crabmeat or raw shrimp or scallops!).

MAKE IT VEGAN: Skip the seafood and honey, and use vegan mayo. Consider adding tofu or seitan.

PREP TIME	15 MINUTES
COOK TIME	8 TO 10 MINUTES
YIELD	4 TO 6 SERVINGS

Dad's Saucy Egg, Beef, and Gai Lan Stir-Fry

Growing up, my dad cooked for the family about once a week. Despite his experience as a line cook in Belgium and Montreal, he wasn't exactly a culinary genius at home. Dad, if you're reading this in heaven, just remember how you excelled at playing chess and mah jong, betting on horses, and helping me win gold for my science projects from elementary all the way to high school and how much I loved and still love you 🖤 ... So even if your cooking was sometimes less stellar, that's okay! (Remember your bitter pasta swimming in white wine? EEK!)

This dish, however, was an exception, the one dish my dad made that I absolutely adored and yearn for. I'm re-creating it here from taste memory, and I can't help but wish we had cooked it together when I was younger. Instead, I chose video games or chatting with friends on AIM while Dad prepared his go-to dish for my baby sister and me. Oh Dad, your dish was colorful, packed with nutrients, and paired perfectly with plain rice. It was testament to a loving father who always did his best. You were the best, Dad.

FOR THE STIR-FRY:

1 pound (454 g) flank steak, sliced across the grain ⅛- to ⅙-inch (3 to 4 mm) thick

Neutral oil for stir-frying

1-inch (2.5 cm) ginger, peeled and sliced

3 garlic cloves, sliced (Dad always sliced his garlic)

8 ounces (544 g) *gai lan* (Chinese broccoli), washed and cut into 2- to 3-inch (5 to 7.5-cm) segments

2 large eggs, beaten

FOR THE BEEF MARINADE:

1 recipe Lai Ching's Go-To Marinade (page 34)

FOR THE SAUCE:

1 tablespoon (15 ml) Shaoxing wine (I suspect Dad added more)

1 tablespoon (15 ml) sesame oil

1 tablespoon (13 g) sugar

½ teaspoon white pepper

1 teaspoon soy sauce

1 teaspoon Chinkiang vinegar

1 teaspoon cornstarch mixed with 2 teaspoons water to form a slurry

Dash of MSG (optional)

FOR THE OPTIONAL TOPPINGS:

Sesame seeds

Fried garlic or shallots

1. Marinate the beef or protein. Make 1 batch Lai Ching's Go-To Marinade in a bowl or container and add the beef (or your protein of choice). Stir with chopsticks or massage to fully coat everything. Cover and refrigerate for at least 30 minutes.

2. If you'd like to velvet the beef or protein before stir-frying, refer to the technique on page 16. If not, proceed to the next step.

3. Mix all the sauce ingredients together in a small bowl. Set aside.

4. Preheat the wok (or frying pan or skillet) over medium-high heat. When it begins to smoke, add about 2 tablespoons (30 ml) neutral oil. Add the ginger and garlic and once they become aromatic (around 30 seconds), introduce the beef. Stir-fry for 1 to 2 minutes before adding the gai lan. Continue to stir-fry until the beef has browned on both sides and the gai lan is vibrant and shiny. If needed, add a bit more oil or a splash of Shaoxing wine to deglaze the wok.

5. Stir the sauce (as the cornstarch may have settled) and pour it around the perimeter of the wok. Quickly stir-fry to mix everything. Once the sauce has thickened slightly, drizzle in the beaten eggs and remove the wok from the heat. Give a gentle stir to avoid overcooking the eggs.

6. Add the optional toppings, if desired. Serve and temper with white rice or plain noodles, as the dish can be quite savory.

(Hope you're proud of this, Dad. Here's to your enduring culinary legacy!)

TIP: *Feel free to swap the beef with another protein. You can also blanch the gai lan before stir-frying.*

PREP TIME	25 MINUTES
COOK TIME	15 MINUTES
INACTIVE TIME	30 MINUTES OR LONGER
YIELD	4 TO 6 SERVINGS

MAKE IT VEGAN: Pick a plant-based protein instead of the beef, use vegan oyster sauce, and omit the eggs.

Chinese Barbecue Pork (Char Siu)

Honestly, few dishes epitomize Cantonese cuisine quite like char siu, or Chinese barbecue pork. Regally adorning Chinatowns worldwide, char siu, with its sticky molasses and honey-glazed, charred red look, is a visual and gustatory delight—glorious food porn, a feast for the eyes. A bowl of rice adorned with succulent char siu slices, Ah Gong's Perfect Wok-Fried Eggs (page 112), and oil-blanched vegetables are my idea of culinary heaven. Moreover, char siu pairs beautifully with soup noodles, milk bread toast, rice noodles, dumplings, and THW Char Siu Bao (page 56). And despite its grandeur, it's not difficult to make char siu at home—the key lies in the marinade and precise oven or air fryer cooking.

FOR THE MARINADE:

2 tablespoons (30 ml) hoisin sauce

1 tablespoon (15 ml) rice vinegar

1 tablespoon (8 g) cornstarch

1 teaspoon miso

2 tablespoons (40 g) honey or agave syrup

2 tablespoons (30 ml) soy sauce

1 tablespoon (15 ml) Shaoxing wine

¼ cup (60 g) packed brown sugar

1 tablespoon (15 ml) sesame oil

3 garlic cloves, minced (or 1 teaspoon garlic powder)

Dash of MSG or 1 teaspoon chicken bouillon powder (optional)

1 drop red food coloring gel or 1 tablespoon (12 g) red yeast rice powder (optional)

FOR THE PORK:

1½ pounds (680 g) fatty pork butt or pork shoulder, sliced into 2- to 3-inch (5- to 7-cm) thick strips

About 1 tablespoon (18 g) salt

1 teaspoon white pepper

1 teaspoon five-spice powder

FOR GLAZING THE CHAR SIU:

2 tablespoons (40 g) molasses or honey mixed with 1 tablespoon (15 ml) hot water

1. Make the marinade by combining all the marinade ingredients in a large bowl or a lidded container.

2. Tenderize the pork by gently pounding with a meat mallet or rolling pin, careful not to flatten it excessively. Season with salt, white pepper, and five-spice powder, rubbing them into the pork. Place the pork in the bowl or container, add the marinade, and massage well. Refrigerate and marinate for at least 2 hours or overnight.

3. Preheat the oven to 400°F (200°C) with a rack in the center. Add about 1 cup (235 ml) water to a roasting pan. Alternatively, create a makeshift roasting pan by placing a wire rack on top of an aluminum-lined baking sheet. Reserve the marinade and roast the pork on the roasting pan for 15 minutes.

4. Combine the glazing mixture with the marinade. Baste the pork with this mixture, ensuring to coat both sides evenly. Rotate the pan and continue baking until the internal temperature reaches 145°F (63°C), another 15 minutes. If you prefer a more charred look, place the pork on the upper oven rack and broil on high for a few minutes. Be cautious to avoid over-burning; aim for a charred look, not a blackened crisp.

5. After removing the pork from the oven, let it rest for a few minutes before slicing. Enjoy with rice, noodles, or toast, or incorporate it into dishes like fried rice or my THW Char Siu Bao (page 56).

TIP: *While the vibrant red color is a char siu signature, you can skip the food coloring gel, or opt to use the red yeast rice powder if you can find it.*

PREP TIME	15 MINUTES
COOK TIME	35 MINUTES
INACTIVE TIME	4 HOURS TO OVERNIGHT
YIELD	1½ POUNDS (680 G) OF CHAR SIU

THE SHARING TABLE

"Sharing the same meal reaffirms kinship."
—*Deng Ming-Dao*

There's a reason why I began this book with a simple bowl of rice. A single grain, among countless others, comes together to create a fulfilling meal, embodying the spirit of unity and community. This is a philosophy central to my Chinese heritage and echoed across many Asian cultures, epitomized by the principle of 一汤三菜 (*yī tāng sān cài*), meaning "one soup, three dishes." This concept finds a parallel in the Japanese culinary tradition of Ichiju Sansai, "one soup, three sides."

What makes 一汤三菜 and Ichiju Sansai so compelling are the diverse flavors and textures they bring to the table for everyone to enjoy together. Consider my Clay Pot Taiwanese Three-Cup Chicken (page 100). The rich, intense flavors of this dish enhance one's experience of a simple bowl of rice. A plate of blanched bok choy, Mapo Tofu (page 104), and a simple broth, or miso soup, would complete the meal: one soup, three dishes, plus rice.

And instead of the three-cup chicken, you could make the Braised and Candied Pork Belly (红烧肉) (page 108) or my family favorite, my Cantonese-Style Stir-Fried Chicken Ding (鸡丁) (page 110).

Having the Koreatown Spicy Tofu Stew (Sundubu Jjigae) (page 102) at the sharing table is perfect too. It offers a spicy soup balanced by the soft tofu and complements rice. It's a comforting meal, made better when shared with others, and paired with other dishes, like my kimchi fried rice and Korean pancakes.

Adding to this mix is Beverly Moore's Chicken Tinola (page 118) and Anh Lam's Vietnamese Sour Noodle Soup (page 106). These comforting and nourishing dishes, made by mothers for their families, speaks volumes about the warmth and love that good food can bring to a home. Plus, they're perfect for sharing.

Thus this chapter is more than just a list of recipes; it's an invitation to gather and connect. It's about enjoying each bite while laughing over shared moments, and relishing the companionship that communal dining brings. So get ready and let's gather around the sharing table.

Clay Pot Taiwanese Three-Cup Chicken

When the clock hits 5 p.m., and I still don't know what to make for dinner (you see a pattern here, right?), I feel a slight panic and break into a sweat. As a New Yorker for more than three decades, anxiety comes naturally to me. But then I take a deep breath and collect myself. For inspiration, I often reflect on the delicious meals I've enjoyed at restaurants. I consider dishes Jake and Philip love, and ones that stand out to me, like a three-cup chicken-flavored hot pot at a local Taiwanese restaurant called Boiling Point.

Jake kept raving about the flavor of the three-cup chicken and how it reminded him of one of his favorite Filipino dishes, chicken adobo. I experimented with flavor combinations and came up with this super easy and humble clay pot dish, inspired by Taiwanese three-cup chicken and chicken adobo. I hope you enjoy it!

FOR THE SAUCE:

1½ tablespoons (22 ml) soy sauce

1½ tablespoons (22 ml) dark soy sauce

1½ tablespoons (22 ml) michiu or rice wine

1 tablespoon (13 g) brown sugar

1 teaspoon rice vinegar or Taiwanese black vinegar

3 bay leaves (optional, but recommended)

Dash of black pepper (optional)

Dash of MSG (optional)

FOR THE CHICKEN:

About 1 pound (454 g) or 4 boneless chicken thighs (skin-on or skinless, your choice), cut into bite-size cubes

Salt and pepper to taste

2 tablespoons (30 ml) sesame oil

6 whole garlic cloves

½-inch (1 cm) ginger, peeled and sliced

Shaoxing wine for deglazing, as needed

FOR THE OPTIONAL TOPPINGS:

Sesame seeds

Scallions, chopped

Thai basil leaves (while this is optional, recipe tester Claire Fan feels a handful is recommended, as "the basil completes and rounds out the flavor of the whole dish")

1. In a bowl, mix together all the sauce ingredients. Set aside.

2. Season the chicken with salt and pepper, keeping in mind that the sauce will be flavorful.

3. Heat a clay pot (or a Dutch oven, heavy saucepan, wok, or frying pan) over medium-high heat until hot, about 2 minutes. Add the sesame oil, garlic, and ginger. Stir until the garlic turns golden, approximately 1 to 2 minutes. Add the chicken and cook until all sides are golden brown, a few minutes.

4. If the chicken sticks to the pot, deglaze it with a splash of rice wine. Add the sauce mixture and stir to combine all the ingredients.

5. Lower the heat to medium-low and cover the pot with its lid. Simmer the chicken for 15 minutes.

6. Remove the lid and stir the chicken to thoroughly coat it with the sauce. If you find the sauce too runny or thin for your taste, mix 1 teaspoon cornstarch with 2 teaspoons water to make a slurry. Add the slurry to the pot and stir. Simmer until the sauce thickens to your desired consistency, coating the spoon or chicken, 1 to 2 minutes.

7. Add the optional toppings such as sesame seeds, chopped scallions, and Thai basil leaves. Serve hot with rice or noodles.

NOTE: This dish is called three-cup chicken because of its three main ingredients and their matching ratios: sesame oil, rice wine, and soy sauce. But don't worry; we won't be using a full cup of each sauce ingredient here.

TIP: Alternatively, you can roast the chicken for 18 minutes at 420°F (215°C), then broil until a nice char develops, about 2 minutes.

PREP TIME	**15 MINUTES**
COOK TIME	**20 MINUTES**
YIELD	**4 SERVINGS**

Koreatown Spicy Tofu Stew (Sundubu Jjigae)

I can't remember when I first had *sundubu jjigae* (silken tofu stew). Was it in my twenties in the early 2000s, at my first job as an "office lady" when I had lunch in NYC Koreatown with my coworkers? Or was it earlier than that, in the late 1990s (gasp!), when my parents first allowed teenage Kat to hang out with her friends in Flushing's Koreatown? (Friends for nearly three decades now!) Either way, there hasn't been a bubbling *ddukbaegi* of sundubu jjigae that I didn't want to slurp up. I also love how this dish can be

customized. Meat lovers can add meat, Spam, or bacon. Seafood lovers can add baby oysters or clams. Vegans can keep this dish vegan. As for me, I'm not picky; as long as the broth is hot and smoky, the silky tofu is flavorful, and there's rice on the table, I'm happy.

P.S.: I know this is not an "authentic" method or an *ahjumma*'s way of making sundubu jjigae. It's my way of making one of my favorite Korean dishes.

Neutral oil for frying

8 ounces (226 g) protein of choice, like shrimp, ham, or scallops

½ onion, diced

4 garlic cloves, chopped

1 teaspoon minced ginger (optional)

2 tablespoons (34 g) gochugaru or 1 to 2 tablespoons (15 to 30 g) gochujang (adjust to taste)

⅓ cup (weight varies) any vegetable or protein of choice, chopped (optional)

¼ cup (60 g) chopped kimchi (optional)

2 tablespoons (30 ml) soy sauce

1 tablespoon (15 ml) Shaoxing wine

2¼ cups (530 ml) dashi or substitute with vegetable or chicken broth

Salt and pepper, to taste

1 teaspoon sugar

Dash of MSG (optional)

Two 16-ounce (453 g) blocks silken tofu (it's also okay to use less tofu if you want)

2 large pasteurized eggs (optional)

3 scallions, chopped

Sesame seeds (optional)

1. Preheat a saucepan, Dutch oven, or *ddukbaegi* over medium-high heat. Once hot, add 1 tablespoon (15 ml) oil and then the protein of choice. Stir-fry until lightly browned all over, for a few minutes. Remove from heat and set aside.

2. In the same cookware, heat 2 tablespoons of oil over medium heat, then add the onion, garlic, and optional ginger. Stir and cook until the onions turn translucent, about 3 minutes. Add the gochugaru or gochujang and stir and cook until fragrant, 1 to 2 minutes.

3. Add the optional vegetables and kimchi, stir, and cook until the veggies are lightly browned, for a few minutes, before adding the soy sauce and Shaoxing wine to deglaze the cookware. Pour in the broth and raise the heat to high. Add the salt and pepper, sugar, and the optional MSG. Once the broth bubbles, add the tofu.

4. Reduce the heat to low. Gently break the tofu into large chunks using a spoon or chopsticks. Avoid mashing the tofu into small bits; it will appear curdled and less appealing if you do. If you feel there's not enough broth, add a little hot water. Allow the tofu to simmer to absorb the flavors from the smoky hot broth, 5 minutes.

5. Add the precooked proteins, stir, and cook for 1 to 2 minutes.

6. Lastly, add the optional eggs and cook for 1 to 2 more minutes before topping with the scallions and optional sesame seeds. Serve immediately.

TIP: Traditionally, sundubu jjigae is made and served in a ddukbaegi, an earthenware pot used as both cookware and serveware for many boiled Korean dishes. I have not yet invested in a ddukbaegi; I usually cook this dish in my saucepan or clay pot. You can also use a Dutch oven.

PREP TIME	**30 MINUTES**
COOK TIME	**30 MINUTES**
YIELD	**4 SERVINGS**

MAKE IT VEGAN: Use vegan dashi or vegetable broth, skip the eggs, and choose plant-based proteins if adding to the stew.

Mapo Tofu
（麻婆豆腐）

I've always found the name of this legendary dish fascinating. "Mapo" is a combination of two Chinese words, "ma" (麻) and "po" (婆), which together means "pockmarked or pock-faced grandma (or old woman)." It's often said that this dish is named after Mrs. Chen, who ran a small restaurant in Chengdu, the capital of Sichuan Province, sometime in the late 1800s. Mrs. Chen had facial scarring due to smallpox; as a result, she was rather unflatteringly nicknamed "Mapo."

Mrs. Chen was known for her spicy and flavorful tofu, which she created to cater to the tastes of her spice-loving customers, both laborers and businessmen alike. The dish became so popular that it eventually (and crassly) took after her nickname, "Mapo." Today, mapo tofu is a beloved and easily one of the most recognizable dishes in China and beyond, known for its bold flavors and spicy kick. *I hope I do your recipe justice here, Mrs. Chen, and thank you for giving generations after generations a comforting and delicious dish to enjoy over and over again.*

FOR THE SAUCE:

1 to 2 tablespoons (17 to 34 g) doubanjiang, adjust to taste

1 teaspoon soy sauce, adjust to taste

1 tablespoon (15 ml) Shaoxing wine

1 tablespoon (13 g) sugar, adjust to taste

½ teaspoon Sichuan peppercorns, toasted and ground

½ teaspoon chili flakes (optional)

½ teaspoon *douchi* (fermented black beans—optional but recommended)

FOR STIR-FRYING:

1 tablespoon (15 ml) neutral oil

3 garlic cloves, minced

1 small onion, finely diced

8 ounces (227 g) fat ground pork, beef, or chicken, or ground plant-based protein

½ cup (120 ml) chicken broth

1 pound (454 g) soft or silken tofu, cut into 1-inch (2.5 cm) cubes

FOR THE CORNSTARCH SLURRY:

1 teaspoon cornstarch mixed with 2 teaspoons water

FOR OPTIONAL GARNISH:

2 scallions, chopped

PREP TIME	**15 MINUTES**
COOK TIME	**20 MINUTES**
YIELD	**4 SERVINGS**

1. Make the sauce by combining the sauce ingredients. Give it a taste and adjust as needed. Set aside but close by.

2. Preheat the wok until it begins to smoke over medium-high heat. Add the oil and once the oil is hot, relatively quickly, add the garlic and onion. Stir and cook until the onion is translucent, a few minutes.

3. Add the ground meat (or protein) to the wok and stir-fry until browned, a few minutes.

4. Stir in the prepared sauce and cook until the flavors have melded, 1 to 2 minutes.

5. Carefully add the broth and tofu to the wok. Bring the mixture to a boil. Reduce the heat to medium and simmer until the tofu is heated through, about 6 minutes.

6. Stir in the cornstarch slurry and cook until the sauce has thickened to your desired consistency, 1 to 2 minutes. Try not to stir too vigorously to prevent the tofu from breaking. Instead, gently fold the tofu into the sauce to keep the pieces intact.

7. Garnish with the scallions, if desired, and serve hot with white rice.

TIP: *For added color, feel free to add green peas or edamame while adding the broth and tofu.*

MAKE IT VEGAN: Use vegetable broth instead of chicken broth, and use ground plant-based protein, such as Beyond Meat or Impossible Plant-Based Beef Ground, or omit the ground meat all together.

NOTE: Substitute the chicken with cooked fish like sea bass, carp, salmon, tilapia, or snapper, if you'd like to enjoy this soup with fish instead. Pan-fry the fish first until cooked before adding it to the noodles, then ladle in the soup. If you can't find greenbrier, you can use celery instead, as Anh has in the past. As for tamarind soup mix, Anh recommends the Knorr brand, or substituting with lemon or lime juice if you can't find it in the stores. Finally, you can also buy prefried tofu puffs in Asian supermarkets and use those instead of making your own fried tofu.

Anh Lam's Vietnamese Sour Noodle Soup (Bún Canh Chua)

At the conclusion of the Vietnam War, Anh Lam, her husband, and their children spent six months in an Indonesian refugee camp before immigrating to the United States. For years, Anh missed the ingredients and flavors of her homeland, Vietnam, as she could not find familiar Asian ingredients in the local markets. It wasn't until she and her family moved to Seattle, Washington, where they discovered the International District and multiple Asian grocery stores, that Anh was able to cook dishes like *canh chua* and *pho* again, without using substitutions. Back in Vietnam, Anh prepared canh chua with snakehead fish. As many of her children did not enjoy fish, she started using chicken instead and even turned canh chua into a main entrée (noodle soup) instead of a side dish by adding *bún* (vermicelli noodles). Thus, a completely new dish was born, Anh Lam's Bún Canh Chua.

Over the years, Anh perfected her recipe and added fried tofu. "It absorbs the soup and tastes amazing when you bite into it," Meiju Ong, Anh's daughter, states. "This soup is a family favorite, and it was important for me to document it for myself and for future generations to come."

RECIPE SPECS

FOR THE FRIED TOFU:

32 ounces (907 g) firm tofu, dried and cut into bite-size cubes or rectangles

Neutral oil for frying

FOR THE OPTIONAL *TÔM KHÔ HÀNH KHÔ PHI* (CRISPY DRIED SHRIMP WITH ONION FLAKE TOPPING):

Neutral oil for frying

1.7 ounces (50 g) dried shrimp

¾ cup (45 g) fried onion or shallot flakes

FOR THE SOUP:

2 chicken breasts, boiled and shredded

2 tablespoons (24 g) chicken powder

2 tablespoons (30 ml) fish sauce

1 teaspoon salt, adjust to taste

2½ tablespoons (30 g) cumin powder

3½ teaspoons (10 g) Knorr Tamarind Soup Mix or 1 tablespoon (7 g) tamarind powder

1½ tablespoons (20 g) sugar or rock sugar

8 ounces (140 g) canned pineapple chunks or fresh pineapple cut into ¾-inch (2 cm) chunks

3 large tomatoes, cut into eighths

¾ pound (336 g) *bạc hà* (greenbrier stalks), with the outer layer peeled and the stalks cut into ¼-inch (6 mm) pieces

1 pound (450 g) vermicelli noodles, soaked and cooked according to the packaging instructions

12 ounces (340 g) bean sprouts

FOR THE OPTIONAL TOPPINGS:

1 bundle of fresh Thai basil

Small chilies, chopped

PREP TIME	20 MINUTES
COOK TIME	35 MINUTES
YIELD	4 TO 6 SERVINGS

1. Make the fried tofu. In a frying pan or heavy saucepan, add enough oil to cover the tofu and deep-fry or shallow-fry the tofu until thoroughly golden brown. Place on a paper towel–lined plate to remove the excess oil and cool. (If you want to skip frying the tofu, that's okay, or you can substitute with premade tofu puffs.)

2. Make the tôm khô hành khô phi. In a small or medium saucepan, add about ⅓ cup (80 ml) neutral oil and heat over medium-high. Once the oil is hot, add the dried shrimp and onion flakes, stir, and cook until slightly golden. Drain the oil and set aside to cool.

3. Make the soup. In a 6-quart (6 L) pot, add about 6 cups (1.4 L) filtered water and bring to a boil. Add the chicken breasts and cook over medium-high heat, about 8 minutes, until cooked. Remove the chicken and set aside to cool.

4. Skim off the impurities or foam that rises to the surface of the pot after boiling chicken. Add the chicken powder, fish sauce, salt, cumin powder, tamarind soup mix, sugar, fried tofu, and pineapples and cook, covered, over medium-low heat for 10 minutes. Meanwhile, shred the chicken and add it, along with the tomatoes, bạc hà, and bean sprouts, to the pot and cook, covered, for 5 minutes. Give the soup a taste and adjust the flavor accordingly with more salt, pepper, fish sauce, or sugar, as needed. If you love sour soups, add more tamarind soup mix.

5. Divide the cooked noodles evenly amongst 4 to 6 serving bowls. Ladle in the soup. Each bowl should also include some of each ingredient in the pot of soup: tofu, bean sprouts, chicken, pineapples, tomatoes, and bạc hà. Top with Thai basil, chili pepper, and a spoonful of tôm khô hành khô phi.

THANK YOU, *Meiju, for sharing your mom's beautiful story and recipe with us.*

Anh Lam or "Ah Ma"

Braised and Candied Pork Belly (红烧肉)

While crafting this book, I asked Subtle Asian Baking members to share their fondest food memories. Gunawan Wu wrote to me: *"During one Chinese New Year when I was working abroad in Australia, my mother cried and said I couldn't enjoy all the delicious food they were having back in Indonesia. She forgot I was a chef, cooking and tasting delicious food every day. But to be honest, no restaurant food can ever replace my mom's home cooking, especially her braised pork belly. She would cook it on special occasions and tell me, 'Eat up and grow up to be a successful man.'"* Today Gunawan enjoys a plethora of accolades and success as an award-winning chef and restauranteur.

Gunawan, your mom proudly watches you, among the stars.

RECIPE SPECS

12 to 16 ounces (340 to 454 g) skin-on pork belly, chopped into bite-size pieces

Salt and pepper to taste

3 garlic cloves, chopped

3 slices ginger

Neutral oil for frying

1 to 2 tablespoons (13 to 26 g) rock sugar

A few teaspoons (15 ml) Coke, Pepsi, or sweet herbal tea from a can

FOR THE SAUCE:

1 tablespoon (15 ml) soy sauce

1 tablespoon (15 ml) dark soy sauce

1 teaspoon black vinegar

1 to 2 star anises

2 to 3 bay leaves, optional

Pinch of cinnamon

2 cups (470 ml) water or chicken broth or veggie broth

FOR TOPPING:

Chopped scallions (optional)

Sesame seeds (optional)

NOTE: This recipe is dedicated to Ju Luk Luan's memory.

Gunawan Wu and his beloved mother, Ju Luk Luan

1. Bring enough water to submerge the pork belly to a rolling boil in a saucepan, pan, or wok. Blanch the pork belly until a layer of white foam floats up to the top, a few minutes. Strain the pork and optionally run it under cold water. Season the pork with salt and pepper.

2. Preheat the wok (or skillet or frying pan) over medium-high heat until it begins to smoke before adding 1 to 2 tablespoons (30 ml) neutral oil. Add the garlic and ginger. As the aromatics sizzle, add the pork belly and stir-fry until lightly browned on both sides, a few minutes.

3. Remove the pork belly and aromatics from the wok and set them aside. Add 2 tablespoons (30 ml) neutral oil and the rock sugar to the wok and cook over low heat. Once the sugar is slightly melted, mix in the soda or herbal tea, add back the pork belly, and stir to coat with the sugar syrup.

4. Raise heat to medium and add the soy sauce, dark soy sauce, black vinegar, star anise, optional bay leaves, cinnamon, and broth or water. Stir and cover with a lid. Simmer for about 45 minutes, stirring every 10 minutes and checking to see if the heat needs to be lowered.

5. Toward the end of cooking, remove the lid and raise the heat to high. Reduce the sauce further, until it's glistening and thick. Remove from heat immediately at this point. Overcooking will result in the sauce separating, with a layer of oil forming.

6. Top with optional toppings, as desired. This dish pairs well with white rice, blanched leafy green veggies, and a soft-boiled egg on the side.

TIP: When trying to re-create his mom's recipe from memory, Gunawan noted down kecap manis (sweet soy sauce), oyster sauce, five-spice powder, garlic, light soy sauce, and dark cooking caramel to include in his braising liquid. I provide you with a basic recipe here, so please experiment to see what flavors you'll come up with and enjoy most. This way, you'll make your very own recipe to remember and one day, pass down.

MAKE IT VEGAN: *Please refer to the Beautifully Braised Mushrooms with Savory Ginger recipe on page 42.*

PREP TIME	**15 MINUTES**
COOK TIME	**45 TO 60 MINUTES**
YIELD	**4 TO 6 SERVINGS**

Cantonese-Style Stir-Fried Chicken Ding (鸡丁)

This dish always transports me back to my childhood home in Coney Island. My mother, after a long day of work, would marinate the chicken overnight and leave instructions for me to steam or fry it with mushrooms and lap cheong for dinner the following evening. The resulting dish is hearty and deeply comforting, with the steaming hot chicken packed with flavor from the umami-rich shiitake mushrooms and the fragrant and salty-sweet lap cheong. It's the type of dish that can nourish anyone after a long day away from home.

While we usually serve the chicken with plain white rice, I've incorporated it into my Hong Kong Clay Pot Rice recipe on page 124. I encourage you to experiment with different ingredients, such as sliced peppers, ham, cashews, or other ingredients that will complement the chicken.

1 recipe Lai Ching's Go-To Marinade (page 34)

4 chicken boneless thighs or about 1 pound (450 g) chicken thighs or breasts, cubed

2 tablespoons (30 ml) neutral oil

About 6 garlic cloves

½- to 1-inch (1 to 2.5 cm) ginger, peeled and sliced or minced

8 to 10 rehydrated shiitake mushrooms, sliced

2 to 4 lap cheong (Chinese sausages), diced

Shaoxing or rice wine for deglazing

4 scallions, chopped

Sesame seeds for garnish (optional)

1. Prepare Lai Ching's marinade following the instructions on page 34. Marinate the chicken for at least 30 minutes, or up to overnight.

2. Velvet the marinated chicken, following the instructions on page 16.

3. Preheat the wok over medium-high heat until it begins to smoke before adding the neutral oil.

4. Add the garlic and ginger to the wok. Once the garlic turns golden, add the mushrooms and lap cheong and stir-fry until the mushrooms are golden and the lap cheong are shiny and fragrant, about 3 minutes.

5. Add the chicken and increase the heat to high and stir and toss constantly. Use Shaoxing or rice wine to deglaze the wok as needed.

6. Continue cooking until all sides of the chicken are golden brown. Deglaze the wok with more Shaoxing or rice wine as needed.

7. Add most of the chopped scallions (reserving some for garnish) and stir well. Remove the wok from heat and transfer the contents to a serving plate.

8. Garnish with the remaining scallions and optional sesame seeds. Enjoy this dish with white rice and a drizzle of *Fire* Chili Crisp Oil (page 176) or Fiery Hot Mayo (page 174), if desired.

NOTE: *Dry shiitake mushrooms take at least 30 minutes to rehydrate, so please plan accordingly.*

PREP TIME	**30 MINUTES**
COOK TIME	**50 TO 60 MINUTES**
INACTIVE TIME	**30 MINUTES**
YIELD	**4 SERVINGS**

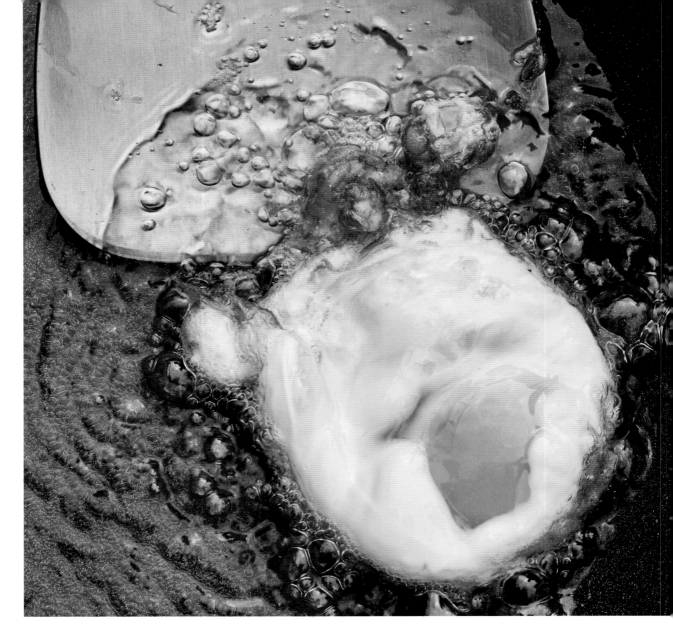

Ah Gong's Perfect Wok-Fried Eggs (Hou Bao Daan)

On rainy days, which are quite common in Seattle, and whenever I think of Ah Gong, my maternal grandfather, I heat up my wok and fry an egg, just like he used to do. Ah Gong's *hou bao daan* (which translates to "pocket or wallet egg") were umami bombs fried to perfection, and his way of saying "I love you, dear grandchild." I'd drizzle a little soy sauce or Maggi liquid aminos and sesame oil over the egg and enjoy it with white rice, milk bread toast, or instant noodles. At times, I'd add a dollop of butter directly to the rice, mixing everything together with the sauce, butter, and runny yolk creating a beautiful blend in the bowl. Each bite? Pure heaven. Indeed, the simplest of meals are often the most comforting and delicious, don't you agree?

4 large eggs

Salt

White pepper

Soy sauce or Maggi liquid aminos

FOR THE OPTIONAL TOPPINGS:

Sesame oil for drizzling

Furikake

Sesame seeds or chopped scallions

Fire Chili Crisp Oil (page 176)

Fried garlic or fried shallots

1. Crack each egg gently into a separate small bowl.

2. Preheat the wok over medium-high heat until it begins to smoke. Add about 3 tablespoons (45 ml) neutral oil, or enough to line the bottom. Allow the oil to heat up for about 10 seconds, then gently slide in the eggs. Depending on the size of your wok or pan, you can cook 1 or 2 eggs at a time. If cooking multiple eggs, try to give each egg some space.

3. Season the eggs with salt and white pepper. Swirl the wok or pan to let the oil coat the eggs. Drizzle soy sauce or Maggi liquid aminos and, if desired, sesame oil over the eggs. Once the edges turn golden brown and crispy, fold the egg whites over the yolk (like folding it in half) to form a "wallet" or "pocket"—hence the name hou bao daan. If you prefer, leave the eggs as they are for a sunny-side-up/overeasy look.

4. Serve the eggs over rice or noodles, drizzling more soy sauce over the top if you like, and adding any desired optional toppings.

TIP: You can also try frying the egg in flavored oil, like chili oil or scallion oil, instead of neutral oil. For a bit of acidity, add a little rice vinegar or Chinkiang vinegar to your fried eggs.

PREP TIME	5 MINUTES
COOK TIME	A FEW MINUTES
YIELD	4 SERVINGS

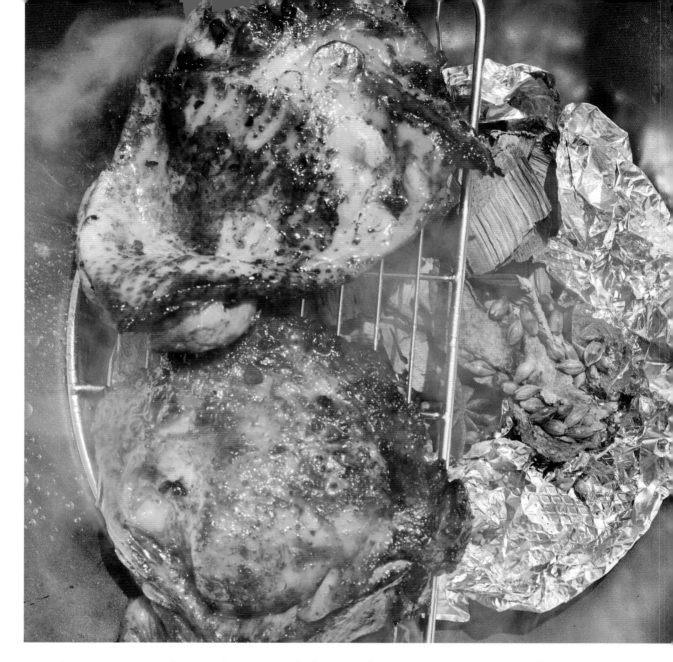

Barley Tea and Cocoa-Smoked Chicken

Unsurprisingly, this is one of my favorite recipes in this book. You'll be amazed at how simple it is to infuse your proteins with profound smoky flavors. All you need is a wok, a steamer rack or bamboo steamer, and ingredients like barley tea, spices such as Sichuan peppercorns and star anise, and don't forget the cocoa powder. Tea smoking, a culinary technique born centuries ago in Sichuan Province, beautifully infuses food with the smoky flavors of tea and spices. I highly encourage you to experiment with different ingredients for the tea blend. I'm planning to try black sesame and matcha next!

RECIPE SPECS

4 skin-on, boneless chicken thighs (about 1 pound or 450 g)

Neutral oil for frying

FOR THE MARINADE:

3 tablespoons (45 ml) dark soy sauce

2 tablespoons (30 ml) granulated sugar

2 garlic cloves, minced

1 tablespoon (8 g) cornstarch

Dash of white pepper

1½ teaspoons minced shallot

A few crushed Sichuan peppercorns (optional)

1 teaspoon sesame oil

3 tablespoons (45 ml) Shaoxing wine

FOR THE SMOKE BLEND:

¼ cup (50 g) roasted barley, the kind used for tea (jasmine, red, green, or black tea leaves can work too)

¼ cup (50 g) granulated or brown sugar

About 3 tablespoons (35 g) uncooked rice grains

2 star anises

A few dried orange peels, if you have them

A few pieces of hickory or apple wood chips, if you have them

½ teaspoon Sichuan peppercorns, crushed

1 tablespoon (7 g) cocoa powder

FOR TOPPING:

Chopped scallions or cilantro (optional)

Sesame seeds (optional)

1. Combine all the marinade ingredients in a bowl or container. Add the chicken and ensure it is thoroughly coated with the marinade. Cover and refrigerate for at least 1 hour.

2. Prepare the smoke blend by mixing all the ingredients together in a small bowl. Fold a sheet of aluminum foil into a makeshift box or cup and add the smoke blend to it.

3. Preheat the wok over medium-high heat until it starts to smoke. Add 1 to 2 tablespoons (15 to 30 ml) neutral oil and fry the chicken thighs on medium heat for about 4 minutes per side. The marinade will thicken, resembling a dark barbecue sauce. Alternatively, deep-fry the chicken until cooked through, a few minutes.

4. Remove the chicken from heat and place it on a greased steamer rack or parchment paper–lined bamboo steamer.

5. Heat a clean wok over medium heat, add the aluminum foil with the spice blend, and let it smoke. As the smoke starts to rise, add the chicken and cover the wok. Let it smoke for about 5 minutes before flipping the chicken to smoke for another 5 minutes.

6. Remove from heat, slice, and serve, topped with optional toppings if desired. Enjoy this flavorful smoked chicken! Save the smoky spice blend for next time.

TIP: I cook outdoors. If you are making this dish indoors, turn on your hood range and crack open the windows. The smoke can be quite intense and linger, making clothes, furniture, hair, and pets all smell smoky-delicious.

PREP TIME	10 MINUTES
COOK TIME	ABOUT 20 TO 25 MINUTES
INACTIVE TIME	AT LEAST 1 HOUR
YIELD	4 SERVINGS

MAKE IT VEGAN: Try tea smoking plant-based proteins like firm tofu, mushrooms, or seitan.

Shanghai Cafe Stir-Fried Yellow Eel

Years ago, my mom, Evelyn, and I would explore NYC's Chinatown every Sunday, picking a spot for lunch. One of our favorite haunts was the now-closed Shanghai Cafe, famous for its soup dumplings and a dish we always ordered: stir-fried yellow eel served over a bowl of hand-pulled noodles and soup. In crafting this recipe, I've aimed to re-create those flavors from memory. The tang of black vinegar, the umami depth from soy sauce and possibly oyster sauce, the rich aromatics, and especially the yellow chives, all melded perfectly with the sweet, delicate eel. Just note that preparing eel can be a bit challenging due to its slimy and bloody nature. I recommend finding deboned eel, preferably prewashed and cleaned, at your local market. Serve this dish with white rice, udon, instant noodles, or bread, and prepare to enjoy second helpings, just like we did at the Shanghai Cafe.

1 pound (454 g) yellow eel, cleaned and deboned

2 scallions, chopped

5 to 6 garlic cloves, chopped

2 tablespoons plus 1 teaspoon (15 g) ginger, minced

About 2 tablespoons (30 ml) neutral oil for stir-frying

1 ounce (28 g) yellow chives, cut into 2-inch (5-cm) segments

1 tablespoon (15 ml) Shaoxing wine

Chili flakes (optional)

Sesame seeds (optional)

FOR THE MARINADE:

1 tablespoon (15 ml) Shaoxing wine

White pepper and salt, for seasoning (be generous with the white pepper)

2 teaspoons cornstarch

1 tablespoon (15 ml) sesame oil

FOR THE SAUCE:

1 tablespoon (15 ml) dark soy sauce

1 tablespoon (15 ml) soy sauce

1 teaspoon oyster sauce

1 teaspoon Chinkiang vinegar

1 teaspoon MSG or chicken bouillon powder

½ teaspoon white pepper

1 tablespoon (13 g) sugar

FOR THE CORNSTARCH SLURRY:

1 teaspoon cornstarch mixed with 2 teaspoons water until combined

FOR DRIZZLING:

1 tablespoon (15 ml) neutral oil

PREP TIME	20 MINUTES
COOK TIME	ABOUT 10 MINUTES
YIELD	4 SERVINGS

1. Blanch the eel in a pot or saucepan of nearly boiling water for about 30 seconds. Remove and rinse under cold water, scraping off any sliminess. Pat dry, cut into 3-inch (7-cm) segments, and then slice into ½-inch (1-cm) wide strips.

2. Make the marinade by combining the marinade ingredients in a bowl. Add the eel, ensuring it is well coated. Set aside.

3. Prepare the sauce by combining all sauce ingredients in a separate bowl. Set aside.

4. Preheat a wok over medium-high heat until it starts to smoke. Add the oil and stir in half of the garlic and all of the ginger. Once fragrant, add the marinated eel.

5. Stir-fry until the eel is lightly browned, a few minutes. Add the yellow chives and Shaoxing wine, and stir for another minute. Pour the sauce around the perimeter of the wok. Toss and stir to coat the eel evenly. Add the cornstarch slurry, and once the sauce thickens to your liking, remove from heat. Note that if the sauce has a thickness to your liking prior to adding the slurry, you can skip adding the slurry.

6. Arrange the eel on a serving dish, creating a well in the center for the remaining garlic and scallions. Heat the drizzling oil in a small saucepan until hot and pour over the garlic and scallions. Stir everything well. Sprinkle with chili flakes and sesame seeds if desired and serve immediately.

TIP: *If you can't find eel or prefer not to use it, you can substitute it with shrimp, razor clams, pork or chicken (cut into thin strips), seitan, sliced shiitake mushrooms, or strips of firm tofu.*

Beverly Moore's Chicken Tinola

Longtime Subtle Asian Baking member and friend Derriel Shine shared this traditional Filipino chicken and soup recipe with me, one her mother, Beverly Moore, had passed down. "This is my mother's recipe, a comfort dish she made for my sister and me growing up. I love this recipe because it's one of the fondest food memories I have with Mom, plus the flavors from the ginger and spinach are amazing! Anytime we felt sick or it was cold outside, Mom would always make this for us, and it has remained a high-demand dish in our household. When I started my own family, this was one of the recipes I made sure I got from her so I can make it for my husband and son . . . they love it! Hope you love it too, Kat!" I love it, indeed, Derriel! Thank you!

RECIPE SPECS

1 pound (454 g) mixed chicken (drums, thighs, breasts, and/or wings, your choice)

1 teaspoon salt for seasoning

2 tablespoons (30 ml) olive oil

1 small onion, chopped

1½ inches (3.8 cm) ginger, peeled and sliced

4 garlic cloves, sliced

2 cups (470 g) chicken or vegetable broth

Salt and pepper to taste

2 tablespoons (30 ml) fish sauce

1 chayote, washed, peeled, and cut into bite-size cubes

2 jalapeños, sliced (optional)

8 ounces (227 g) baby spinach, washed (spinach is okay too but chop it up first)

1. Season the chicken by rubbing it with salt.

2. In a heavy saucepan or wok over medium-high heat, add the olive oil. Once hot, add the onion, ginger, and garlic. Cook until aromatic and the onions turn golden and translucent, about 3 minutes.

3. Add the chicken and sauté until browned on both sides, a few minutes.

4. Pour in the chicken or vegetable broth. Bring the mixture to a boil, then reduce the heat to low. Season with additional salt, pepper, and fish sauce to taste. Add the chayote and optional jalapeños. Cover and let it simmer until the chayote is tender, about 15 minutes.

5. Stir in the spinach, letting it wilt in the hot broth for about a minute. Serve immediately while hot, ideally with a side of rice. Be sure to slurp the soup.

NOTE: *You can use bok choy instead of spinach and squash, zucchini, or green papaya instead of the chayote. This is, by the way, a soupy dish.*

PREP TIME	20 MINUTES
COOK TIME	30 MINUTES
YIELD	4 SERVINGS

Derriel Shine and her mother, the lovely Beverly Moore

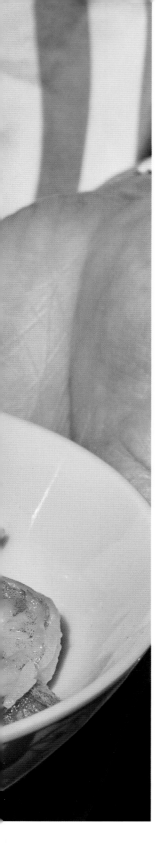

THE RICE IS RIGHT
米

*"Rice is great if you're really hungry
and want to eat 2,000 of something."*
—*Mitch Hedberg*

My friend, are you ready to "rice and shine" with all the comforting and tantalizing recipes in this chapter? After all, rice is always right. What other food can you eat by the thousands and not feel guilty (or well, explode)? We'll start things off with Bibimbap Your Way (page 122), where you'll assemble a rice dish that will satisfy all your cravings at once. Bibimbap holds a special place in my heart; when I was pregnant and working in Koreatown in NYC, I enjoyed bibimbap almost every day. (You can find out more about that in the recipe's headnote!) Moving on from stone pot rice, we'll venture into Hong Kong Clay Pot Rice (page 124), with a recipe that will hopefully convince everyone to embrace their "clay pot era."

This chapter wouldn't be complete without some fried rice dishes, and I've included two for you. First, we have the classic and iconic Yangzhou Fried Rice with Furu Sauce (page 126), a dish that never disappoints. Second, for those who love a bit of heat, I've added a spicy, melty Cheesy Kimchi Fried Rice (page 128).

I couldn't write a chapter on rice without featuring my Cozy, Comfy Congee (page 134), the ultimate comfort food for the soul. I believe this chapter will "rice to the occasion" whenever you're in need of nourishment. I bet you'll love all these "rice-cipes" here! Even if you don't, I'll still wish you a "rice" day! 🫙 Okay, I'll stop with the puns now, before someone complains *a-grain*.

Bibimbap Your Way

During my pregnancy, I consistently craved bibimbap, especially *dolsot bibimbap*. My body instinctively knew how nutritious this flavorful dish was, with its colorful, visually appealing mix of veggies, proteins, and the pop of red and spice from gochujang. It made Philip dance in my belly.

As long as you practice mise en place, you can have a delicious, satisfying homemade bibimbap ready in about an hour! Assemble the bibimbap to your liking, omitting or adding ingredients as you see fit. Topping it off with a fried egg truly seals the deal, in my honest opinion. (If you have pasteurized eggs, you can crack a raw one directly onto the hot rice and other ingredients, mix well, and enjoy!)

2 cups (400 g) uncooked short-grain white rice or jasmine rice

½ cup (70 g) sliced chicken or any other sliced protein of choice

Neutral oil for frying

1 teaspoon minced garlic

1 teaspoon minced ginger

4 large eggs

Sesame seeds (optional)

A handful of chopped scallions (optional)

Gochujang, soy sauce, and sesame oil on the side

FOR THE MARINADE:

1 tablespoon (15 ml) sesame oil

1 tablespoon (15 ml) soy sauce

1 tablespoon (13 g) sugar

1 teaspoon Shaoxing wine

Dash of black pepper

FOR THE VEGETABLES (OR USE WHATEVER VEGGIES YOU'D LIKE):

½ cup (230 g) bean sprouts

⅓ cup (37 g) thinly sliced or julienned carrots

⅓ cup (37 g) thinly sliced or julienned zucchini

½ cup (23 g) sliced shiitake mushrooms

½ cup (90 g) cooked spinach or Waifu's Spinach Gomae-ae (page 50)

1. Cook the rice according to the instructions on page 24.

2. In a bowl, combine the marinade ingredients. Add your choice of sliced protein and marinate for at least 30 minutes.

3. Preheat a wok or frying pan over medium-high heat until it begins to smoke. Add about 1 tablespoon (15 ml) neutral oil, followed by the garlic and ginger. Cook until aromatic, about 15 to 30 seconds. Add the marinated protein and cook until browned on all sides, about 2 minutes. Remove from heat and set aside.

4. Add more oil to the pan or wok if necessary. Stir-fry the vegetables (individually or together) until they're tender or wilted, about 2 to 3 minutes for the carrots, zucchini, and mushrooms, and 1 to 2 minutes for the spinach and bean sprouts. Set aside.

5. To fry the eggs, heat a frying pan or skillet over medium heat and add 1 tablespoon (15 ml) neutral oil (or butter). Crack the eggs into the pan, ensuring there's enough space between them, and lightly season with salt, pepper, and soy sauce. Cook until the egg whites are set and crispy but the yolks are still runny, about 2 minutes. If using pasteurized eggs, you could also try mixing a raw egg with the hot rice and ingredients instead of frying the egg.

6. Assemble the bibimbap. Divide the rice evenly between 4 medium bowls (or small dolsots, if you have them). Artfully arrange the protein and vegetables on top of the rice in each bowl, topping each with a fried egg. Sprinkle optional sesame seeds and chopped scallions on top. Alternatively, you can assemble all the ingredients in 1 large bowl. Serve with gochujang, soy sauce, and sesame oil on the side. Be sure to mix everything together so each bite has a little of everything.

NOTE: *With dolsot bibimbap, cooked rice and other ingredients are assembled in a dolsot (a stone pot made with a soft stone called agalmatolite) and baked in the oven until a crispy layer of rice forms at the bottom. It's common to pour hot water over the scorched, crispy rice, serving it as a browned rice tea or soup after the meal.*

TIP: I highly recommend adding gochujang sauce to the bibimbap and mixing everything together before eating.

PREP TIME	20 MINUTES
COOK TIME	40 MINUTES
YIELD	4 SERVINGS

Hong Kong Clay Pot Rice

I haven't met a soul who doesn't love clay pot rice. The crispy, crackling rice on the bottom is a treasure after enjoying all the fluffy, flavorful rice on top. Here I recommend adding Cantonese-Style Stir-Fried Chicken Ding (page 110) to the rice, but feel free to add any cooked toppings of choice, like my Dim Sum–Style Steamed Spare Ribs (page 68), Beautifully Braised Mushrooms with Savory Ginger (page 42), steamed lap cheong, or stir-fried pork or beef. Everything about this dish spells love and comfort, and cooking in a clay pot somehow makes me feel connected to my ancestors.

2 cups (400 g) uncooked jasmine rice or short-grain white rice

1½ cups (352 ml) water

½ cup (120 ml) chicken or vegetable broth

1 tablespoon (15 ml) sesame oil

FOR THE SAUCE:

2 tablespoons (30 ml) soy sauce

1 tablespoon (15 ml) dark soy sauce

2 teaspoons granulated sugar

Dash of MSG

1 tablespoon (15 ml) Shaoxing wine

1 teaspoon fish sauce (optional)

1 tablespoon (15 ml) sesame oil

FOR THE CHICKEN DING:

1 recipe Cantonese-Style Stir-Fried Chicken Ding (page 110)

FOR THE TOPPINGS:

Sesame seeds

Chopped scallions

1. Rinse the rice in a fine-mesh sieve under cold water until the water runs clear.

2. Lightly grease all sides of a clay pot with a neutral oil using a pastry brush, then preheat it over medium heat.

3. Combine the rinsed rice, water, broth, and sesame oil in the clay pot. Bring the mixture to a boil over medium-high heat, keeping the lid off so you can monitor the liquid's state. Once it's boiling, reduce the heat to low, cover with the lid, and simmer for 18 to 20 minutes, or until the rice is tender and all the liquid has been absorbed. You'll know the rice is cooked when steam ceases to escape from the hole in the clay pot's lid.

4. While the rice cooks, prepare your sauce. Combine all sauce ingredients in a small bowl and set aside.

5. Also while the rice is cooking, prepare a batch of chicken ding.

6. After the rice is fully cooked, remove the lid and taste a small amount of rice to verify it's cooked through. If it's gritty, the rice needs more time. Once cooked to satisfaction, fluff the rice with a rice paddle or fork.

7. Distribute the Chicken Ding evenly over the rice and drizzle the prepared sauce over everything. Cover and cook on low heat for a few more minutes.

8. Garnish with optional sesame seeds and chopped scallions. Serve immediately.

9. After serving, for those who want to enjoy the crispy rice stuck to the bottom of the clay pot, pour in hot water or hot black tea and let everything steep for a few minutes. The resulting flavorful rice tea and soaked rice pieces are a delight to savor!

NOTE: *This was recipe tester Claire Fan and her family's favorite recipe. "The chicken came out super tender, and the rice cooked perfectly with the light sesame flavor."*

TIP: *I have only cooked this dish in a clay pot; I'm told it's doable in a Dutch oven and rice cooker, but I just haven't tried yet.*

PREP TIME	30 MINUTES
COOK TIME	45 MINUTES
YIELD	4 SERVINGS

Yangzhou Fried Rice with Furu Sauce

My all-time favorite fried rice dish is Cantonese salted fish and chicken fried rice (鹹魚雞粒炒飯). However, Yangzhou (or Young Chow) fried rice, with its colorful presentation and versatile ingredients, often has broader appeal. Legend even suggests fried rice originated in Yangzhou, so there you have it.

In this dish, feel free to add, omit, or modify ingredients to satisfy your taste buds. Once you master frying rice, the possibilities become endless. Keep in mind, the key to excellent fried rice is using dried-out rice. Day-old or overnight rice seems to provide the best texture and consistency. Although using freshly cooked rice is possible, if you cook it with less water or dry it out for a few hours, I haven't dared to try that yet!

FOR THE FURU SAUCE:

2 teaspoons furu (or fermented tofu)

1 teaspoon soy sauce

2 teaspoons mirin, honey, or agave syrup

Dash of brown or granulated sugar

1 teaspoon Shaoxing wine

2 teaspoons water

½ teaspoon sesame oil

FOR THE FRIED RICE:

Neutral oil, for frying

2 large eggs, beaten

1 small or medium onion, minced

12 medium deveined, peeled, and cooked shrimp (optional, but recommended)

6 ounces (170 g) char siu, diced (optional, but recommended)

6 ounces (170 g) Virginia ham or sliced ham, diced (optional, but recommended)

1 cup (132 g) frozen mixed vegetables (corns, peas, carrots, your choice), thawed

Splash of Shaoxing wine

4 cups (800 g) cooked white rice, preferably day-old or overnight and dry

Salt and white pepper, to taste

Dashes of MSG (optional)

1 to 2 cups (55 to 110 g) chopped iceberg or romaine lettuce

3 scallions, chopped

1. Combine all the furu sauce ingredients in a small bowl and set aside.

2. Preheat a wok or frying pan over medium-high heat until it begins to smoke. Add about 2 tablespoons (30 ml) neutral oil and the beaten eggs. Scramble until cooked, then remove the eggs, chop up into smaller pieces, and set aside.

3. In the same wok or frying pan over medium-high heat, add 2 tablespoons (30 ml) neutral oil before adding the onion. Cook until the onion is translucent. Then, add the shrimp, char siu, ham, and veggies. Toss the ingredients as you stir-fry for approximately 2 minutes, until the vegetables soften. Add a splash of Shaoxing wine and stir-fry for another minute.

4. Add the cooked rice to the pan and use a spatula or wooden spoon to break up any clumps. If needed, drizzle in 1 tablespoon (15 ml) neutral oil to ensure the rice becomes shiny and is thoroughly heated. Add the furu sauce, pouring it in around the perimeter of the wok (if you're using one) to help evenly distribute the sauce. Quickly stir-fry, mixing everything together.

5. Add the chopped eggs and stir. Season the fried rice with salt, white pepper, and MSG if using. Finally, add the lettuce and scallions, give everything a quick stir, and serve immediately.

TIP: Customize this recipe by adding, omitting, or substituting different proteins and vegetables to your liking. You can use bacon, pancetta, or lap cheong instead of ham, seitan instead of char siu, and add edamame or snow pea shoots instead of the veggie medley.

NOTE: To address clumpy rice, place it in a large bowl, drizzle about 1 tablespoon (15 ml) neutral oil over it. Then, with food-safe gloves on, crumble the rice to break up the clumps and separate the grains.

"This recipe was life-changing."

—*Chi Nguyen, recipe tester
and SAB member*

PREP TIME	**25 MINUTES**
COOK TIME	**15 TO 20 MINUTES**
YIELD	**4 SERVINGS**

Cheesy Kimchi Fried Rice

This dish is a family favorite. Jake loves the crispy, spicy, taste bud–tantalizing fried rice, especially when it's on the oilier side, and I can't resist picking at the melty cheese with my chopsticks. Cheesy kimchi fried rice is the ideal weeknight meal, especially when you find leftover rice and kimchi in the fridge. Having both cabbage and radish kimchi readily available is a must in our household. As a fermented food, kimchi provides a potent source of probiotics and nutrients and boasts a long refrigerator shelf life. More than that, it elevates any fried rice dish with its unique flavor, satisfying crunch, and welcome fiber boost.

FOR THE SAUCE:

1 tablespoon (13 g) sugar or honey

1 tablespoon (15 ml) Shaoxing wine

2 tablespoons (30 ml) soy sauce

1 tablespoon (15 ml) sesame oil

½ tablespoon gochujang (optional)

FOR THE FRIED RICE:

Neutral oil, for frying

1 onion, minced

5 garlic cloves, chopped

⅓ to ½ cup (50 to 75 g) chopped protein of choice (like bacon, ham, brisket, tofu, Spam, pork belly, chicken, or shrimp)

1 cup (150 g) chopped kimchi or vegan kimchi (use more if you'd like)

½ cup (75 g) chopped radish kimchi (optional, but nice for an added crunch)

4 cups (740 g) cooked white rice, preferably day-old or overnight, and dry (crumble first if too clumpy)

Salt and pepper to taste

Dash of MSG (optional)

1 cup (150 g) shredded mozzarella, cheddar cheese, or your favorite cheese—add more or less according to preference

FOR THE OPTIONAL FRIED EGGS:

4 large eggs

Neutral oil or 1 tablespoon (13 g) unsalted butter

Salt, pepper, soy sauce to taste

FOR THE OPTIONAL TOPPINGS:

1 to 2 tablespoons (5 to 10 g) grated Parmesan cheese, more if you'd like

Sesame seeds

2 to 3 scallions, chopped

Crumbled or shredded nori

1. Combine all sauce ingredients in a small bowl and set aside.

2. Preheat a wok or skillet over medium-high heat until it starts to smoke. Add about 2 tablespoons (30 ml) neutral oil, followed by onion and garlic. Lower the heat to medium and cook until the onion becomes translucent, a few minutes.

3. Increase the heat to medium-high, add your chosen protein, and stir-fry until golden brown.

4. Stir in the kimchi and radish kimchi, continuing to stir-fry until fragrant. Push all the ingredients to the pan's edges, add the rice, and gently flatten with a spatula. Season the rice with salt, pepper, and optionally, MSG. Allow the rice to fry undisturbed for a minute.

5. Mix all the ingredients and add the sauce around the wok's perimeter (or drizzle over the rice if using a skillet pan). Stir well and increase the heat to high. Flatten the rice again and cook for another minute, or until a crust forms at the bottom.

6. Lower the heat to medium-low and add the cheese on top. Cover with a lid and let the cheese melt. Alternatively, broil the cheese and rice until the cheese melts and forms a crust, as per recipe tester Lingjie He's recommendation.

7. For the optional fried eggs, heat a frying pan or skillet over medium heat and add neutral oil or butter. Crack the eggs, ensuring there's space between them, and season lightly with salt, pepper, and soy sauce. Cook until the eggs' bottom sets and turns crispy while the yolks remain runny. Top each rice bowl with a fried egg. Garnish with your desired toppings and portion the rice into 4 serving bowls and serve immediately.

NOTE: While the combination of melty egg and cheese is divine, you may omit the fried egg if it seems too indulgent. However, recipe tester Mindy Cheung and her husband firmly believe that the fried eggs are essential.

PREP TIME	15 MINUTES
COOK TIME	15 MINUTES
YIELD	4 SERVINGS

Suraj's Cashew Upma with Chutney Powder

This recipe is another gem from my dear friend Suraj Chetnani, who never fails to delight us with delicious home-cooked meals. (Do check out his lemongrass chai recipe in *Modern Asian Baking at Home*!) After considering various options, Suraj chose to share his upma recipe. "It's a super simple dish with countless variations," he remarked. Having grown up in Mumbai, Suraj savors fond memories of relishing upma for breakfast alongside a cup of chai. Now, as a busy father, he often prepares this dish as a midday snack or a nutritious breakfast for his son, Gian. This filling meal can even be enjoyed for dinner, particularly when paired with protein-rich chutney pudi, a spiced peanut powder. It's comfort food that packs a surprisingly rich flavor.

FOR THE OPTIONAL CHUTNEY PUDI:

1 cup (145 g) peanuts

2 tablespoons (19 g) sesame seeds

1 teaspoon cumin seeds

1 teaspoon coriander seeds

2 sprigs curry leaves

5 to 8 dry Kashmiri chilies or any dry red chilies, adjust to taste

1 teaspoon sugar

½ to 1 teaspoon salt, adjust to taste

3 to 5 garlic cloves

FOR TOASTING THE SEMOLINA:

1 cup (75 g) fine semolina (or rava)

FOR THE UPMA:

2 tablespoons (30 ml) neutral oil or ghee (or clarified butter)

½ onion, minced

1 teaspoon black mustard seeds

Pinch of asafetida (aromatic Indian spice)

12 to 16 cashews

2 to 3 dry Kashmiri chilies or any dry red chilies

8 sprigs curry leaves

3 cups (705 ml) water

1 teaspoon salt (adjust to taste)

6 ounces (170 g) vegetable medley (like chopped carrots, pea, green beans, and corn)

½ lemon or lime

Chopped coriander (optional)

1. Make the optional chutney pudi a few days in advance or the night before. Dry-roast the peanuts and sesame seeds in a frying pan over low heat until golden and fragrant, stirring occasionally. Set aside. Dry-roast the cumin, coriander seeds, curry leaves, and chilies in the same pan for a few minutes. Once cooled, combine these ingredients with sugar and salt in a food processor or mortar and pestle, blending or grinding into a powder. Add peanuts, sesame seeds, and garlic cloves, grinding until the mixture is powdery. (Avoid overblending, as this will cause the peanuts to release oil.) Store in an airtight container and set aside.

2. Toast the semolina in a saucepan over medium heat, stirring constantly for about 2 to 3 minutes. Remove from the pan and set aside.

3. In the same saucepan, heat 2 tablespoons (30 ml) neutral oil or ghee over medium heat. Add the minced onion and cook until translucent. Add the mustard seeds, asafetida, and cashews, stirring for about 20 seconds. Next, add the chilies and curry leaves, cooking for another 20 to 30 seconds. Stir in the water and salt. Mix in the vegetable medley and cook until softened. Raise the heat to high and bring the mixture to a boil.

4. Gently stir in the semolina, reducing heat to low. If the mixture appears too dry, add a little water. Cover the saucepan and stir intermittently every 10 to 15 seconds to prevent or break up clumps. Cook for a few more minutes before removing from heat.

5. Squeeze lemon or lime juice over the upma and mix well. Garnish with optional coriander. If desired, stir in a dollop of ghee or butter while the upma is still hot. Serve with spoonfuls of chutney pudi, if available.

TIP: Suraj suggests adding toppings like chopped green chilies, ketchup, or green chutney for extra zing.

Celebrating our dear friends, Suraj and Grace

PREP TIME	5 MINUTES
COOK TIME	10 MINUTES
YIELD	2 TO 4 SERVINGS

Hong Kong Cafe–Style (Cha Chaan Teng) Baked Pork Chop and Rice

This dish is a classic found in the bustling Hong Kong *cha chaan teng* (literally "tea restaurant," but more akin to a café or diner). Likely developed in the mid-1900s, it represents an early fusion of East-meets-West gastronomy. Tender pork chops lie atop a bed of fried rice, nestled beneath a blanket of melty cheese, all brought together by a hearty, sweet pastalike tomato sauce. This culinary masterpiece exemplifies

why my mother misses Hong Kong, with its food as vibrant as its skyline, orchestrating a symphony of flavors, and delighting with its harmonious fusion of cultures. Suffice it to say, I too adore this dish.

FOR THE MARINADE:

4 teaspoons (20 ml) Worcestershire sauce

4 garlic cloves, minced

4 teaspoons (20 ml) soy sauce

½ teaspoon celery salt (optional)

1 teaspoon salt

4 teaspoons (20 ml) Shaoxing wine

1 tablespoon (13 g) granulated sugar

4 teaspoons (20 ml) sesame oil

1½ tablespoons (12 g) cornstarch

Dash of white or black pepper

Dash of MSG (optional)

FOR THE PORK CHOPS:

About 1 pound (454 g) pork chops (about 5 thin-cut, or 3 thick-cut; choose the fattier ones)

½ cup (60 g) all-purpose flour

FOR THE EGG FRIED RICE:

2 tablespoons (30 ml) neutral oil

2 large eggs, beaten with ½ teaspoon soy sauce

4 cups (800 g) cooked white rice

⅓ cup (43 g) frozen vegetable medley (corn, peas, string beans, carrots), thawed

Salt and pepper to taste

2 teaspoons soy sauce

Dash of MSG (optional)

FOR THE TOMATO SAUCE:

1 tablespoon (15 ml) neutral oil

1 small onion, sliced

2 small tomatoes, cut into wedges

3 garlic cloves, chopped

¼ cup (60 g) ketchup

2 tablespoons (30 ml) Worcestershire sauce

2 teaspoons granulated sugar

White or black pepper to taste

1 teaspoon salt

Dash of MSG

¾ cup (175 ml) water

1 teaspoon cornstarch

FOR TOPPING:

About ½ cup (60 g) mozzarella or melting cheese of your choice (optional, and add more if you'd like)

PREP TIME	**35 MINUTES**
COOK TIME	**ABOUT AN HOUR, TOTAL**
INACTIVE TIME	**2 HOURS OR LONGER**
YIELD	**4 SERVINGS**

1. Make the marinade by combining all the ingredients in a mixing bowl.

2. Pound the pork chops with a mallet or rolling pin, until thinner but not mushy. Add the pork chops to the marinade, ensuring they are fully coated. Cover and refrigerate for at least 2 hours.

2. Preheat the oven to 375°F (190°C) with a rack in the center.

3. Make the egg fried rice. Heat 2 tablespoons (30 ml) neutral oil in a pan over medium-high heat. Add the beaten egg and scramble it. While the egg is still wet, add the cooked white rice and vegetable medley, and stir to combine. Add the soy sauce, salt, pepper, and the optional MSG. Stir and cook until the rice glistens (add a little more oil as needed) and the veggies are tender, a few minutes. Set aside.

4. Cook the pork chops. Dredge each marinated pork chop in the all-purpose flour, ensuring each is well coated. Heat 4 tablespoons (60 ml) neutral oil in a pan over medium-high heat. When the oil is hot, sear the pork chops until golden brown, 2 to 3 minutes per side. Set aside.

5. Make the tomato sauce. In the same pan, add 1 tablespoon (15 ml) neutral oil. Over medium-high heat, sauté the onion and garlic until fragrant, a few minutes. Add the tomatoes, ketchup, Worcestershire sauce, sugar, pepper, salt, and MSG, mix well, and cook until bubbly, 1 to 2 minutes.

6. In a small bowl, mix the cornstarch with ¼ cup (60 ml) water, then add it to the pan. Stir until the tomatoes soften and the sauce thickens enough to coat a spoon, a few minutes. Taste and adjust the seasoning as needed.

7. Assemble and bake. Spread the egg fried rice in a large baking dish or oven-safe skillet. Place the seared pork chops on top of the rice, and pour over the tomato sauce, ensuring the pork chops are sufficiently coated. If using cheese, sprinkle it evenly over the top.

8. Bake for 15 to 20 minutes, until the pork chops are cooked through and the cheese is melted and bubbly. Allow it to cool for a few minutes before serving.

NOTE: *This dish is a labor of love and not a quick weeknight meal due to several steps and required time.*

Comfy Cozy
Congee

Congee, or *jook* as we call it in Cantonese, is a dish you often don't fully appreciate until you're sick with a nasty cold or stomach bug. At least, that was the case for me, until I moved away from my mother and couldn't have her delicious congee anymore for a few years. Honestly, few dishes are as comforting to me as a good bowl of jook. It's a blank canvas, a rice porridge you can enjoy just plain or with almost any protein or sauce. Liquid rice, LOL. Some prefer a thicker version; I lean toward a smooth and silky texture. My favorite congee is *tang jai jook*, filled with flavorful bites of pork and seafood, and topped with salted peanuts. A close second would be congee with century egg and salted pork. Paired with fresh *youtiao* (Chinese fried dough), congee can be quite heavenly, and always comfy-cozy.

1 cup (200 g) uncooked white rice, short- or long-grain

7 cups (1.6 L) water

1 cup (235 ml) vegetable broth, chicken broth, or dashi

1 teaspoon neutral oil

Up to 1 cup (weight varies) of chopped and marinated protein of choice like chicken, pork, shiitake mushrooms, tofu, or seafood (optional)

Salt and white pepper to taste

1 teaspoon chicken or mushroom bouillon (optional)

Dash of MSG (optional)

FOR THE OPTIONAL TOPPINGS:

Salted, roasted peanuts (recommended)

Julienned ginger (recommended)

Pork floss

Chopped scallions (recommended)

Soy sauce

Fire Chili Crisp Oil (page 176)

Sesame seeds

1. Rinse the rice until the water runs clear. Soak the rice in water for about 30 minutes.

2. In a pot or heavy saucepan, add the water, broth or dashi, and oil and bring to a rolling boil. Strain the rice and add it to the pot or saucepan. Stir constantly while cooking over high heat for 5 minutes. (Mom does this for at least 10 minutes, but I'm considering your arm muscles here!)

3. Reduce the heat to low and let the mixture simmer for 20 to 30 minutes, stirring occasionally to prevent the rice from sticking to the pot. Once the congee has thickened, add your choice of marinated protein and let it cook thoroughly for a few minutes.

4. Season the congee with salt and white pepper, starting with 1 teaspoon salt and adjusting to taste. Add the optional chicken or mushroom bouillon and MSG.

5. Serve the congee hot, topped with your preferred toppings and drizzled with your sauce of choice, or enjoy it as is.

TIP: If you prefer plainer congee, substitute the cup of broth or stock with a cup of water.

NOTE: Experiment with both short- and long-grain rice to see which one you prefer.

PREP TIME	5 MINUTES
COOK TIME	30 MINUTES
YIELD	4 SERVINGS

Chinatown
Hainanese
Chicken and Rice

Childhood Sundays were a culinary adventure in NYC's bustling Chinatown for Mom, Evelyn, and me. Our taste buds would lead us to a hidden Malaysian restaurant, drawn by a heavenly Hainanese chicken and rice. This dish, originating from Hainan, China, pairs tender steamed chicken with fragrant rice cooked in chicken broth and coconut milk. Complemented with an array of condiments such as chili sauces and scallion ginger oil, and served alongside pickled cucumbers, this meal is more than just food; it reminds me of all the wonderful times spent with my family as a child. In fact, it's so comforting and delicious that I wouldn't mind having it on my deathbed.

RECIPE SPECS

FOR THE POACHED HAINANESE CHICKEN:

4 skin-on and boneless chicken thighs (or 2 skin-on chicken breasts)

1 tablespoon (18 g) coarse or kosher salt

2 cups (470 ml) chicken broth

Seasoning such as MSG, white pepper, and salt to taste

1-inch (2.5-cm) ginger, peeled and sliced

2 to 3 garlic cloves

2 scallions, cut into 3-inch (7-cm) segments

Ice water in a shallow bowl for an iced water bath (optional)

FOR THE HAINANESE RICE:

1½ cups (292 g) uncooked short-grain white rice

1½ cups (352 ml) chicken broth

1 teaspoon MSG, chicken bouillon

Pinch of salt

3 to 4 tablespoons (45 to 60 ml) full-fat coconut milk

1 tablespoon (15 ml) rendered chicken fat or canola or rapeseed oil

FOR THE SCALLION GINGER SAUCE:

2 to 3 scallions, chopped

1½ inch (3.8 cm) ginger, minced

½ teaspoon salt

½ teaspoon sugar

1 tablespoon (15 ml) sesame oil

½ teaspoon rice wine vinegar

Dash of MSG (optional)

5 tablespoons (75 ml) neutral oil

FOR THE OPTIONAL GARNISH:

Chopped cilantro

Sliced cucumbers

Chopped scallions

PREP TIME	20 MINUTES
COOK TIME	45 MINUTES
YIELD	4 SERVINGS

1. Make the chicken. Rub salt on the chicken, mimicking an exfoliating spa treatment, then rinse with cold water. In a heavy saucepan, bring water to a boil. Add the chicken and cook briefly until impurities rise to the top, about 2 to 3 minutes. Remove the chicken, discard the water, and clean the saucepan. In the same saucepan, bring the broth, seasoning, ginger, garlic, and scallions to a rolling boil. Add the parboiled chicken, reduce the heat to low, and ensure the chicken is fully submerged in broth. If not, add more water. Cook until the chicken's internal temperature reaches 165°F (73°C) and the juices run clear, roughly 30 minutes. Optional but recommended: Immerse the cooked chicken in an ice water bath for a few minutes to cool, which helps tenderize the meat and improves the skin's texture. Pat the chicken dry, brush with sesame oil, and set aside. Save the chicken broth for later.

2. Make the rice while the chicken is simmering. Rinse the rice thoroughly. In a rice cooker, add all the ingredients for the rice, stir well, and start the cooker. If you don't have a rice cooker, bring the chicken broth, MSG, salt, coconut milk, and oil to a boil in a saucepan. Add the rice, return to a boil, then reduce heat to low and cover. Let the rice simmer until it's tender and all the liquid is absorbed, about 15 to 18 minutes. Remove from heat, keep covered, and let it stand for around 10 minutes. Fluff the rice with a paddle before serving.

3. Make the scallion ginger sauce. Combine all ingredients, except the oil, in a heatproof bowl. Heat the oil in a saucepan until it reaches about 375°F (190°C). Carefully pour the hot oil into the bowl and stir.

4. Assemble the Hainanese chicken and rice. Divide the chicken and rice evenly among the plates. Traditionally, the chicken is chopped before serving. If desired, garnish with cilantro and arrange sliced cucumbers on the side. Ladle the hot chicken broth into 4 bowls and garnish with chopped scallions. Serve with soy sauce, scallion ginger sauce, and sweet Thai chili sauce, or *Fire* Chili Crisp Oil (page 176) on the side for dipping.

TIP: *Consider serving this dish with the scallion ginger sauce plus soy sauce and Thai sweet chili sauce on the side for dipping.*

LIFE IS NOODIFUL

*"Peace will come to the world when the
people have enough noodles to eat."*
—Momofuku Ando

Life is *noodiful* like my Vietnamese Auntie Eva's Pho Gà (page 156)—beautiful
and colorful, comforting you as you slurp the soup, but also stinging a bit when
it's too hot or spicy, and always leaving you feeling bittersweet when you get to
the end and have none left. Noodles, a beloved, versatile, and global staple, are
simple enough to prepare. They can be challenging when it comes to perfecting
their texture (chewy or soft?) and choosing the right noodle shape for each dish.
For instance, rice cakes can be tubular, cubes, or flat oval discs. Ramen noodles,
depending on the broth and pairings, can be thick and wavy or thin and straight.
Don't worry though. I've done all the guesswork for you, and we'll use mainly
store-bought packaged noodles, which usually come with cooking instructions. So
get ready to make my go-to Shanghai Rice Cakes (page 146). The rice cakes are
chewy and charred, and the sauce is umami-ful. If you're having a crappy day and
need something super satisfying and fuss-free, try my easy Asian-style pasta dishes—Chili Crisp Butter Garlic Pasta (page 148) and Kat's Favorite Wafu Pasta (page
154). If you're in the mood for something spicy and quick to make (less than 20
minutes!), don't miss Jamie's Favorite Laksa Noodle Soup (page 158). I developed
this dish for my friend Jamie, who couldn't stop raving about all the laksa she had
during her trip to Singapore, eating it for breakfast, lunch, and dinner! Now she
can always relive her vacation when she makes laksa at home. With my recipes,
you too can explore the rich and delicious world of Asian-inspired noodles. Life is
indeed "noodiful," and perhaps that's why humans have enjoyed noodles for thousands of years, and probably will for thousands more.

Stir-Fried Korean Spicy Rice Cakes (Tteokbokki / 떡볶이)

Tteokbokki, or spicy rice cakes, is a beloved Korean dish commonly found at street food stalls, Asian markets, and Korean households and restaurants. Often served with banchan (side dishes) and topped with boiled eggs, tteokbokki delivers a delightful blend of sweet, savory, and spicy flavors that will tantalize your taste buds.

In creating this recipe, I deviated from the traditional method of cooking rice cakes in a broth made from anchovies and dried kelp. I drew inspiration from one of my favorite dishes at the now-closed Hanjan, a Korean culinary hotspot in NYC, helmed by chef and cookbook author Hooni Kim. Kim's unforgettable crispy tteokbokki, served on a sizzling hot plate, boasted an unmatched level of crispiness that can be challenging to achieve in a wok, without using ample oil. While my version isn't an exact replica of Kim's dish, it's still delicious, rich, and somewhat complex, yet remains easy to prepare—like many of my recipes. A word of caution: You might want to pair this fiery dish with a cold glass of milk or *makgeolli* (a milky rice wine), as the sweet ingredients can be deceiving.

FOR THE SAUCE:

1½ tablespoons (22 ml) soy sauce

3 tablespoons (51 g) gochujang, adjust to taste

3 tablespoons (60 g) honey, agave syrup, or maple syrup, adjust to taste

2 tablespoons (26 g) brown sugar, adjust to taste

2 tablespoons (30 ml) sesame oil

1 tablespoon (15 ml) Shaoxing wine

1 tablespoon (15 ml) hoisin sauce

A little water, as needed, to dilute the sauce

FOR STIR-FRYING:

1 pound (454 g) Korean rice cakes (frozen and cylindrical or tubular)

4 tablespoons (60 ml) neutral oil, for the wok or frying pan

5 garlic cloves, chopped

½ medium onion, sliced

6 ounces (170 g) Korean flat fish cakes (or odeng) cut into bite-size pieces

2 teaspoons duck fat (optional, adds extra richness)

4 scallions, chopped; reserve a third for garnishing

Shaoxing wine for deglazing

FOR GARNISHING:

White or black sesame seeds for garnishing

The reserved chopped scallions

1. Prepare the sauce by combining all sauce ingredients in a small bowl. Set aside for now.

2. Soak the rice cakes in water according to the packaging instructions (usually about 20 minutes), then strain.

3. Preheat a wok or frying pan over medium-high heat until it starts to smoke. Add the oil, followed by the onion and garlic a few seconds later, stirring as they sizzle. Once the garlic turns golden, add the fish cakes (or tofu) and cook until both sides are golden, 1 to 2 minutes. Then, add the rice cakes and the optional duck fat.

4. Stir-fry the rice cakes until slightly crispy and golden brown on both sides, a few minutes. If they stick to the wok or pan, deglaze with a tablespoon of rice wine. Stir in two-thirds of the scallions.

5. Add the sauce and increase the heat to high, continuously stirring and tossing the rice cakes to ensure the sauce evenly coats all ingredients. If possible, perform a pan flip or two with care.

6. Remove from heat and serve piping hot, garnished with sesame seeds and the remaining chopped scallions. Grab your cold drink of choice, fan your lips, and savor the dish!

TIP: *If your rice cakes are sticking too much to the wok, consider adding more oil than suggested in the recipe.*

NOTE: Korean rice cakes are typically vegan and gluten-free. If you can't find *odeng* (fish cakes), you can use any fish cake variety, omit it entirely, or replace it with fried tofu.

PREP TIME	10 TO 15 MINUTES
COOK TIME	15 MINUTES
YIELD	4 SERVINGS

Creamy Dreamy Pumpkin Spice Miso Udon

For the past five years, my family and I have visited the Carpinito Brothers Farm pumpkin patch in Kent, Washington, every October. As the weather turns crisp, I can't help but brainstorm new ways to infuse pumpkin into my baking and cooking. This is particularly fitting during the fall, when pumpkin-spiced creations take center stage. Philip loves udon (and frankly, I'm obsessed too). Since he's not fond of tomato-based sauces, I decided to concoct a pumpkin-based sauce, marrying the comforting subtle sweetness of pumpkin with the umami-richness of miso for this unique dish.

Imagine coming home after a long day, craving something quick, easy, and comforting. In just minutes, you can whip up this sauce, cook the udon with lightning speed, and savor a mouthwatering meal. Don't skimp on the pinch of cardamom in the sauce if possible, and make sure to stock your freezer with a few packs of frozen udon. Found in Asian supermarkets, frozen udon is usually precooked, requiring only a quick dip in boiling water to heat it up.

RECIPE SPECS

FOR THE SAUCE:

1 can (15 ounces or 425 g) pumpkin puree

1½ tablespoons (26 g) miso (or to taste)

2 tablespoons (30 g) unsalted butter

½ cup (120 ml) heavy cream

¼ cup (60 ml) chicken or vegetable broth

1 tablespoon (15 ml) cooking rice wine or Shaoxing wine

Pinch of cardamom

Pinch of nutmeg or cinnamon (optional)

Salt and pepper to taste

FOR THE NOODLES:

2 packets (1 pound or 454 g each) frozen udon

1 tablespoon (14 g) unsalted butter

2 teaspoons soy sauce

1 tablespoon (15 ml) cooking rice wine or Shaoxing wine

Salt and pepper to taste

FOR OPTIONAL GARNISH:

2 tablespoons (18 g) pine nuts

2 tablespoons (18 g) pistachios, deshelled and chopped

Fresh mint or basil leaves

Edible flowers, if you desire

1. Combine all the sauce ingredients in a saucepan and cook over medium heat, stirring continuously until smooth and well-blended. Once the sauce bubbles around the edges, a few minutes, remove it from the heat. Set aside for now.

2. Bring a heavy saucepan of water with 1 teaspoon salt added to a rolling boil over high heat. Gently drop in the frozen udon and cook according to the packaging instructions, which usually takes around 2 to 3 minutes.

3. Strain the udon and rinse under cold water.

4. Melt 1 tablespoon (14 g) butter in a frying pan or wok over medium heat. Add the udon and stir with chopsticks or a spatula. Allow the udon to cook for a minute before drizzling in the soy sauce and wine. Season with salt and pepper to taste, and stir to evenly distribute the seasoning.

5. Add generous dollops of the pumpkin sauce and mix until the sauce thoroughly coats the udon. If there is leftover sauce, store it in an airtight container in the refrigerator for up to 4 days, or freeze for up to 3 months. If using the refrigerated sauce, make sure to reheat it before using.

6. Remove from heat and dish up the udon. Garnish with your choice of optional toppings and serve immediately.

TIPS: If pumpkin puree isn't on hand, whip up a quick and delectable sauce using 1 tablespoon (14 g) melted unsalted butter, 2 teaspoons soy sauce, 1 tablespoon (15 ml) cooking rice wine or Shaoxing wine, ¼ cup (60 ml) heavy cream, and 1 tablespoon (17 g) miso. To add some heat, drizzle any chili crisp oil of your choice. If udon is unavailable, feel free to use any other type of noodles or pasta, as pictured.

PREP TIME	**15 MINUTES**
COOK TIME	**10 MINUTES**
YIELD	**4 SERVINGS**

MAKE IT VEGAN:
Use vegan butter, vegan cream, and vegan vegetable broth. Udon is typically vegan, made with wheat flour, water, and no eggs. To confirm, double-check the label on the packaging.

Auspicious Longevity Noodles
(Yi Mein / 伊面)

During every Lunar New Year and many birthday celebrations, my maternal grandparents would prepare longevity noodles, or *yi mein*. Sometimes, they would keep it simple with just shiitake mushrooms and scallions, while on other occasions, they would feel lavish and add lobster or crabmeat. Flat and absorbent, these noodles are excellent carriers for any sauce, like the rich essence of lobster.

While I enjoy making yi mein noodles from scratch, I honestly recommend purchasing them premade from an Asian supermarket. Homemade yi mein can be fragile and labor-intensive, though using a pasta machine is quite helpful. Longevity noodles also need to be deep-fried and then boiled, so when pressed for time, it's best to opt for store-bought yi mein. Stock up on packs of these versatile noodles, as they are quicker to prepare than dry pasta.

FOR THE SAUCE:

2 tablespoons (30 ml) soy sauce

1 tablespoon (15 ml) dark soy sauce

1 tablespoon (15 ml) vegan or regular oyster sauce

A dash of white pepper

1 tablespoon (15 ml) sesame oil

1 tablespoon (15 ml) Shaoxing wine

1 tablespoon (13 g) brown sugar

THE REST OF THE INGREDIENTS:

3 tablespoons (45 ml) neutral oil, like canola or avocado

About 8 to 12 ounces (230 to 340 g) yi mein noodles (dry)

6 garlic cloves, chopped

½-inch (1 cm) ginger, minced

8 to 10 dried shiitake mushrooms, rehydrated, stems removed, and sliced

5 scallions, cut into 3- to 4-inch (7- to 10-cm) segments (alternatively, use Chinese chives)

Optional proteins (lobster, pork, tofu, or abalone), cooked and chopped, quantity as desired

1. Prepare the sauce by mixing all the sauce ingredients in a small bowl, and set aside for now.

2. Cook the noodles by boiling the dry yi mein noodles for 1 to 2 minutes until they are cooked but still al dente and chewy. These noodles can be fragile, so avoid overcooking them, as you want them to remain long and intact to symbolize longevity. Strain the noodles.

3. Preheat a wok or frying pan over medium-high heat until it begins to smoke. Then, add the neutral oil. Add the ginger and garlic, and once the garlic turns golden, add the mushrooms and optional proteins, if desired. Remember to continuously stir the ingredients at high heat while stir-frying.

4. After the mushrooms develop a golden-brown coating (and your optional proteins are cooked through), add the noodles and stir. Once they are warm and coated with oil, pour in the sauce. Be gentle when stirring the noodles, as they may break.

5. Lastly, incorporate the scallions or chives and cook for about 20 to 30 more seconds before removing the dish from the heat.

6. Serve immediately, as these noodles taste best when piping hot. If you enjoy a bit of a kick, a drizzle of *Fire* Chili Crisp Oil (page 176) or a whopping dollop of XO sauce is the perfect finishing touch.

NOTE: Keep in mind that it takes a few hours for dried shiitake mushrooms to rehydrate in water, so plan accordingly. Although this dish is typically vegetarian, you can customize it by adding proteins like stir-fried lobster, pork, tofu, or abalone. Be sure to fully cook the proteins (added along with the shiitake mushrooms) before incorporating the noodles into the wok or frying pan.

TIP: If you're interested in making yi mein noodles from scratch, visit modernasianbaking.com and search for my homemade yi mein recipe.

PREP TIME	**20 MINUTES**
COOK TIME	**15 MINUTES**
YIELD	**4 SERVINGS**

Shanghai Rice Cakes (Chao Nian Gao / 炒年糕)

I love developing copycat recipes and feel a great sense of achievement when I successfully re-create my favorite restaurant meals at home. This recipe draws inspiration from one of my favorite dishes at Ding Tai Fung (DTF), a world-famous Taiwanese restaurant chain that serves Shanghai soup dumplings and Shanghai rice cakes. What I love about this dish is that it's a complete meal that can be prepared in less than 30 minutes. The base recipe, which doesn't include any meat-based proteins, is both vegan and gluten-free (when you use gluten-free soy sauce). The rice cakes have a chewy texture with a slight crisp and char, and their rich flavors are enhanced with *wok hei*. You'll probably want to make this dish over and over again, experimenting with added shiitake mushrooms or tofu one night, shrimp or pork belly on another, or just the rice cakes and sauce on their own. Have fun personalizing this copycat dish any way you'd like! You can also substitute the rice cakes with thick Shanghai noodles to make *cu chao mian* (Shanghai fried noodles).

3 scallions, chopped into 3- to 4-inch (7- to 10- cm) segments

4 garlic cloves, minced

A small piece of ginger, about 1 inch (2.5 cm), minced

About ½ to 1 pound (227 to 454 g) of any protein of choice, chopped (firm tofu, shrimp, pork, beef, chicken, seitan, or a mix, like the shrimp and pork belly I used for my dish)

About 1 cup (85 g) baby bok choy or napa cabbage, washed, dried, and chopped

About 1 pound (454 g) rice cakes (fresh or dried, available at your local Asian supermarket)

FOR THE SAUCE:

2 tablespoons (30 ml) soy sauce

2 tablespoons (30 ml) dark soy sauce

1 tablespoon (15 ml) oyster sauce

1 tablespoon (15 ml) black sesame oil (you can substitute with peanut oil)

1 tablespoon (15 ml) black vinegar

2 tablespoons (26 g) brown sugar

1 tablespoon (15 ml) Shaoxing, rice, or cooking wine

FOR THICKENING THE SAUCE (OPTIONAL):

Mix 1 teaspoon cornstarch with 2 teaspoons cold water to make a slurry

FOR GREASING THE PAN:

2 tablespoons (30 ml) neutral oil

1. Make the sauce by combining all the sauce ingredients in a bowl.

2. Rehydrate the rice cakes according to the instructions on the packaging. Typically, this involves soaking them in water. Strain and set aside.

3. Preheat the wok (or frying pan or skillet) over medium-high heat until it begins to smoke, then add the neutral oil. Cook the aromatics (scallions, garlic, ginger) until the garlic turns golden, about a minute. Add your protein of choice and cook until slightly browned on all sides, then toss in the bok choy or napa cabbage.

4. Add the rice cakes. Be sure to continuously stir and toss the ingredients while frying. If you find any ingredients sticking too much to the wok or frying pan, deglaze with a splash of cooking or Shaoxing wine.

5. Pour in the sauce (be sure to mix it first, as some sugar may have settled at the bottom of the bowl) around the perimeter of the wok (or drizzle it over the rice cakes if using a pan or skillet) and stir to combine and coat all the ingredients with the sauce. Add the optional cornstarch slurry and stir again.

6. Once the sauce and slurry have thickened and everything is nicely coated with sauce, remove from heat and serve immediately. A little *Fire Chili Crisp Oil* (page 176) or XO sauce pairs well with these rice cakes.

TIP: *Have Shaoxing or cooking wine close by to deglaze the wok as needed while stir-frying.*

PREP TIME	15 MINUTES
COOK TIME	15 MINUTES
YIELD	4 SERVINGS

Chili Crisp Butter Garlic Pasta

This is my subtle Asian twist on the classic Neapolitan staple, the spaghetti aglio e olio. Embrace the flavor explosion, courtesy of taste bud–tantalizing ingredients such as *Fire* Chili Crisp Oil (page 176), oyster sauce, and soy sauce. The blend of umami and spice here never fails to make me drool, and it's no surprise this dish is also one of Philip's favorites! We delight in how easy it is to prepare, then savor it with chopsticks. And seeing my child eagerly lick his plate clean and request seconds reminds me how, in a pinch, sometimes simplicity reigns supreme.

RECIPE SPECS

1 pound (454 g) uncooked spaghetti, fettuccine, linguine, or your pasta of choice

2 tablespoons (28 g) unsalted butter

5 garlic cloves, minced

½ cup (50 g) grated Parmesan cheese

FOR THE SAUCE:

1 teaspoon sesame oil

1 teaspoon oyster sauce

2 tablespoons (40 g) honey, adjust to taste

2 tablespoons (30 ml) soy sauce

2 tablespoons (30 ml) *Fire Chili Crisp Oil* (page 176), adjust to taste

1 tablespoon (15 ml) Shaoxing wine (optional)

FOR THE OPTIONAL TOPPINGS:

1 pasteurized egg

Minced parsley, chives, or scallions

Sesame seeds

Grated Parmesan cheese

1 to 2 teaspoons chili crisp oil, adjust to taste

Black pepper

1. Bring a pot of water with 1 tablespoon (18 g) salt to a boil. Add the pasta and cook according to the directions on the package, until al dente. Reserve about 1 cup (235 ml) of the pasta cooking water, then drain the pasta.

2. Prepare the sauce by combining the sauce ingredients with the reserved pasta cooking water and set aside.

3. Preheat a frying pan over medium heat and add the butter. Once the butter has melted, add the garlic and cook until golden and fragrant, 1 to 2 minutes. Pour in the sauce, stirring frequently, and cook for 1 to 2 more minutes.

4. Incorporate the pasta, mixing well to thoroughly coat it with the glistening buttery brown sauce. Cook until the sauce is reduced to your desired consistency, about 2 minutes. Adjust seasoning as needed.

5. Add the cheese and toss thoroughly. Optionally, crack an egg directly into the center of the pasta and stir. Remove from heat.

6. Transfer to serving dishes and garnish with your desired toppings. I recommend sprinkling on more cheese, adding a drizzle of chili crisp oil, and garnishing the dish with a pop of green from minced chives or scallions.

MAKE IT VEGAN: Substitute butter with vegan butter, use vegan oyster sauce, use agave nectar or brown rice syrup instead of honey, and substitute Parmesan cheese with nutritional yeast. Use only the vegan optional toppings.

PREP TIME	10 MINUTES
COOK TIME	15 MINUTES
YIELD	4 SERVINGS

Sichuan Ants Climbing a Tree
(蚂蚁上树)

This Sichuan noodle dish serves wonderfully as an accompaniment to a bowl of rice or as a satisfying stand-alone entrée. Contrary to what the name suggests, no ants are actually used in the preparation of this dish. The name is derived from the visual of stir-fried minced proteins in brown soy sauce, resembling ants climbing tree branches (the noodles). With its blend of savory, fermented flavors and contrasting textures, this dish is both delightful and a classic, with or without the ants.

¾ cup (100 g) mung bean noodles (glass noodles or cellophane noodles work too)

2 tablespoons (30 ml) neutral oil for stir-frying

3 to 4 garlic cloves, minced

2 teaspoons doubanjiang or spicy fermented bean paste

½ cup (110 g) ground pork (or chicken) or ground plant-based meat, or about ½ cup (120 g) diced or cubed firm tofu, seasoned with salt and pepper

FOR THE SAUCE:

2 teaspoons (30 ml) dark soy sauce

1 teaspoon oyster sauce or vegan oyster sauce

1½ teaspoons brown or white sugar

¼ cup plus 1 teaspoon (65 ml) chicken or vegetable broth

1 to 2 teaspoons sesame oil

1 to 2 teaspoons Shaoxing wine

FOR THE TOPPINGS:

2 scallions, chopped

Black or white sesame seeds (optional)

1. Soak the noodles in hot water for a few minutes, until softened, or follow the instructions on the packaging. Drain and set aside.

2. Make the sauce by combining all the sauce ingredients together in a bowl.

3. Preheat the wok or frying pan over medium-high heat until it begins to smoke. Add the neutral oil, followed by the garlic. Once the garlic is fragrant, mix in the doubanjiang. Add the ground protein (or tofu) and stir-fry until lightly browned.

4. If needed, add a little more cooking oil and a splash of Shaoxing wine for deglazing. Add the noodles and stir-fry until well combined with the protein, about 1 to 2 minutes. Add the sauce by pouring it around the perimeter of the wok (or drizzling it over the noodles if using a frying pan). Constantly stir the noodles, and once they've absorbed all the sauce, the dish is ready.

5. Add the scallions. This step is quick, so be ready to serve immediately, with or without rice, garnished with sesame seeds if desired.

TIP: *I also enjoy preparing a deconstructed, simplified version of this dish. I combine softened noodles, cooked proteins, diced garlic, scallions, and a basic sauce made with doubanjiang, soy sauce, Shaoxing wine, and sugar in a bowl. I then pour hot oil over everything, enjoy the sizzling sound, and mix everything together. I recommend trying either version of this dish.*

MAKE IT VEGAN:
Omit the "ants" and animal proteins and use vegan oyster sauce and vegetable broth.

PREP TIME	**15 MINUTES**
COOK TIME	**15 MINUTES**
INACTIVE TIME	**30 MINUTES**
YIELD	**2 TO 4 SERVINGS**

Curried Vermicelli (Singapore Chow Mei Fun)

This dish is my all-time favorite stir-fried noodle dish, and it most likely originated in southern China (between Hong Kong and Guangzhou, and not Singapore), where Cantonese eateries and street food hawkers and vendors used curry powder and satisfied the growing demand for spicier Southeast Asian flavors. Over time, this dish became a popular street food and food court staple, and now you can order it at almost any dim sum or Cantonese restaurant. Whenever I visit Chinatowns in cities like Vancouver, Hong Kong, Toronto, or NYC, I make sure to find this dish. If I feel nostalgic for the tastes of my childhood or crave something incredibly satisfying and comforting, I make it at home.

FOR THE STIR-FRY:

10 ounces (283 g) dry rice vermicelli noodles

Neutral oil for stir-frying

2 large eggs, beaten

8 ounces (226 g) shrimp, peeled and deveined (optional)

5 ounces (140 g) protein of choice, like shredded or diced ham or char siu, or a mix

1 cup (50 g) bean sprouts

1 cup (150 g) sliced or chopped colorful bell peppers (red, green, yellow)

Splash of Shaoxing wine, for deglazing

2 garlic cloves, minced

2 tablespoons yellow curry paste (30 g) or 1½ tablespoons (9 g) yellow curry powder (if using powder, mix with 2 tablespoons [30 ml] water to form a paste first)

2 scallions, cut into 2- to 3-inch (5- to 7-cm) segments

FOR THE SAUCE:

¾ teaspoon white pepper

1 tablespoon (15 ml) soy sauce

1 teaspoon sugar

¼ teaspoon salt

Dash of MSG (optional)

FOR THE OPTIONAL TOPPING:

Toasted sesame seeds

1. Soak or cook the rice vermicelli noodles according to the packaging instructions until softened. Drain and set aside.

2. In a small bowl, combine all of the sauce ingredients and mix until well blended. Set aside.

3. Preheat a wok or frying pan over medium-high heat until it starts to smoke. Add 2 tablespoons (30 ml) neutral oil and fry the beaten eggs until set. Remove from the pan and cut into shreds.

4. In the same wok or pan, add another 2 tablespoons (30 ml) neutral oil and stir-fry the chosen protein, shrimp (if using), bean sprouts, and bell peppers over medium-high heat until lightly browned, about 3 minutes. Add a splash of Shaoxing wine for deglazing, if desired. Remove from heat and set aside.

5. If needed, clean the pan or wok before preheating it again until it starts to smoke. Over medium-high heat, add another 2 tablespoons (30 ml) neutral oil, then the minced garlic and curry paste. Once aromatic, add the noodles and toss to coat with the curry (noodles should turn yellow). Pour the sauce over the noodles and stir well.

6. Add the cooked eggs, protein, shrimp (if using), bean sprouts, and peppers to the noodles, and toss everything together, 1 minute.

7. Finally, add the scallions, give everything a quick toss, then serve immediately while the dish is piping hot, topped with sesame seeds if desired. *Fire* Chili Crisp Oil (page 176) on the side is optional.

PREP TIME	30 MINUTES
COOK TIME	50 TO 60 MINUTES
YIELD	4 SERVINGS

MAKE IT VEGAN: Omit the eggs or use an egg substitute, use plant-based proteins, and add more vegetables as desired!

Kat's Favorite Wafu Pasta

Mentaiko, or marinated pollock or cod roe, is often spicy and rich with umami and flavor, and surprisingly unfishy. Mixed in this silky and creamy pasta sauce, it's the star, making this dish as comforting as it's craveable. I recommend adding cooked seafood like squid or clams, though tofu or mushrooms would work beautifully as well.

It's no wonder mentaiko pasta is one of Japan's most popular fusion dishes, and this is my favorite wafu pasta.

3 tablespoons (30 to 45 g) unsalted butter or vegan butter

½ medium onion, chopped

4 garlic cloves, minced

½ cup (about 113 g) cooked and chopped protein of choice, like ham, firm tofu, mushrooms, bacon, clams, or squid or a mix (optional)

1½ tablespoons (22 ml) soy sauce

1 teaspoon yuzu or lemon juice

1 tablespoon (15 ml) sake or Shaoxing wine

1 teaspoon mirin or a dash of sugar

2 pieces of mentaiko (pollock roe) with the membrane removed (though I find the membrane is chewy and delicious, LOL)

4 tablespoons (60 ml) heavy cream

Salt and pepper to taste

About 8 ounces (226 g) spaghetti or fettuccine or 1 pound (454 g) frozen udon

1 large pasteurized egg (optional)

FOR THE OPTIONAL TOPPINGS:

Black or white sesame seeds

1 scallion, chopped

Chili pepper flakes

Shredded nori seaweed

Shredded shiso leaf

Tobiko or caviar

1. Preheat a skillet, wok, or pan over medium-high heat. Add the butter and when it's all melted, add the onions. Sauté until golden, a few minutes, before adding the garlic. Stir in the cooked protein of choice, if using, and sauté until hot. Remove from heat and set aside.

2. In a large bowl, combine the soy sauce, yuzu or lemon juice, sake or wine, mirin or sugar, the remaining butter (melted), heavy cream, mentaiko, and salt and pepper. Add the cooked onions, garlic, and optional proteins. Cover and set aside.

3. In a pot of boiling water, add 1 tablespoon (18 g) salt, and cook the spaghetti or fettuccine according to the packaging instructions until al dente. (If cooking udon, frozen udon is ready in about 3 minutes.) Reserve about ¼ cup (60 ml) hot pasta water before draining.

4. Add the pasta to the large sauce bowl and mix. Crack in the egg, if using, while the pasta is still hot. If there isn't enough sauce, drizzle in some of the reserved pasta water before discarding.

5. Garnish with the optional toppings of your choice and serve immediately. It is not recommended to reheat this pasta, as that will overcook the mentaiko; however, if you must, it is okay to pan-fry leftover pasta the next day.

TIP: *If you're short on time, you can make a simpler version of this dish by skipping step 1. This means your pasta won't have cooked onions, garlic, or protein. When making the sauce in step 2, add in 2 tablespoons (30 ml) melted butter. It'll still be super satisfying and delicious.*

PREP TIME	15 MINUTES
COOK TIME	15 MINUTES
YIELD	4 SERVINGS

NOTE: Mentaiko can be found in Asian supermarkets or Japanese grocery stores, or ordered online.

Auntie Eva's Pho Gà

During the pandemic, I hadn't had the chance to see my beloved Auntie Eva and her family in quite some time. When I told them I was coming for a visit, Auntie Eva pulled out all the stops and spent half a day crafting a mouthwatering homemade *pho gà*—a traditional Vietnamese chicken noodle soup—just for me.

I savored every last bite of her delectable creation and imagined this was what Dad loved to eat as a youth in Hanoi. Auntie Eva generously took the time to share her recipe with me, walking me through each step, offering up some of her own personal cooking tips and tricks. It was adorable to see her rave about her favorite brand of fish sauce—"Three Crabs brand!"—and how it's a must to buy in bulk at Costco. It was a truly unforgettable experience that made my first trip to San Francisco memorable.

Though I may not have checked off all the usual tourist sights—the Golden Gate Bridge or the Painted Ladies—I felt more than content just basking in the warmth of Auntie Eva's hospitality and learning about her cherished family recipe. Sharing good food with loved ones is, after all, one of the biggest joys in life.

1 whole chicken, halved, with one half to make 1 recipe Super Juicy and Crispy Baked "Fried" Chicken (page 88)

About 4 servings or 1 pound (454 g) fresh rice stick or pho noodles

FOR THE OPTIONAL SPICE SACHET:

¼ teaspoon ground cloves

¼ teaspoon coriander seeds

¼ teaspoon fennel

¼ teaspoon ground black cardamom

FOR THE BROTH:

2 large onions, halved

1-inch (2.5 cm) ginger, peeled and sliced

A handful of whole star anise (about 6 to 8)

7 cups (1.6 L) water

2 cinnamon sticks

⅓ cup (90 ml) fish sauce

¼ cup (50 g) rock sugar (or 2 tablespoons [26 g] granulated sugar or 3 tablespoons [45 g] brown sugar)

1 teaspoon kosher salt, adjust to taste

2 tablespoons (30 ml) soy sauce

1 tablespoon (6 g) chicken or mushroom bouillon powder

Dash of MSG (optional)

FOR THE OPTIONAL TOPPINGS:

1 cup (50 g) bean sprouts

½ cup (8 g) Thai basil leaves

2 scallions, chopped

¼ cup (4 g) chopped cilantro

½ medium onion, julienned

2 limes, cut into wedges for squeezing

Bird's eye chilis or jalapeño peppers, chopped

Hoisin and sriracha or hot sauce on the side

PREP TIME	15 MINUTES
COOK TIME	1 HOUR, 25 MINUTES
YIELD	4 TO 6 SERVINGS

1. Split the chicken in half. Remove the drumstick and wing from one half. Set this half aside. With the other half chicken and the removed drumstick and wing, make the baked "fried" chicken recipe. Alternatively, you can use the whole chicken in the soup and have shredded boiled chicken as a topping later.

2. Cut the onions into halves and transfer them, along with the ginger and star anise, to a lined baking sheet. Roast at 425°F (220°C) until the onions are golden brown and aromatic; charred is okay but not burnt, about 25 to 30 minutes. Alternatively, air-fry at 400°F (205°C) until golden brown, about 15 minutes.

3. Make the optional spice sachet. Add the optional spice sachet ingredients into a tea sachet or spice sachet.

4. In a large pot, add the water, cinnamon sticks, fish sauce, sugar, salt, soy sauce, bouillon powder, and MSG, if using. Add the roasted onions, star anise, and ginger. Add the optional spice sachet if you made it. Bring to a boil, while occasionally stirring, before adding one half of the chicken. Simmer for 30 minutes before removing the chicken and the white chicken foam. Set the chicken aside to cool. Cover the pot with a lid and cook the broth over low heat for about 2 hours. See the tip for an alternative way to cook the broth.

5. Shred the chicken. If the chicken tastes bland to you, drizzle with some sesame oil, fish sauce, and soy sauce, and mix thoroughly. Set aside.

6. Rehydrate and cook the rice noodles according to the packaging instructions. Fresh pho noodles are quick to prepare, so don't overcook them. Ideally I recommend you rinse the cooked noodles with cold water, then divide them among 4 serving bowls.

7. Assemble the pho gà. Strain the broth first, as the onions will come apart in the soup, then ladle hot, clear broth over the noodles in each bowl. Add the shredded chicken meat and/or pieces of the Super Juicy and Crispy Baked "Fried" Chicken if you prepared it. Garnish with your toppings of choice and serve, piping hot, with a side of lime wedges and sauces.

TIP: An alternative to step 4 is preparing the broth using the manual mode and high pressure of a pressure cooker or Instant Pot for 11 minutes. Remove the chicken and allow it to cool before shredding. Use the manual mode for another 15 minutes to continue cooking the broth. Each time, allow the pressure to release naturally for a few minutes, then quick-release the remaining pressure. Strain the broth and enjoy with noodles. To make beef pho, instead of using chicken, add about 1 pound beef bones or oxtail to the soup or oxtail and serve with sliced eye of round beef marinated with Lai Ching's Go-To Marinade (page 34).

Auntie Eva in Paris, 2023

Jamie's Favorite Laksa Noodle Soup

My friend Jamie Aragonez, co-owner of World Spice in Seattle, texted me pictures of all the food she had during her trip to Singapore, and they were all *laksa*, I kid you not. (Okay, maybe I exaggerated a little!) Her favorite version of this classic dish was found at a local chain named Toast Box. "The velvety coconut broth coated the noodles in deliciously spicy curry. Every spoonful was different, and each bite complemented the next," she told me. "Maybe I'm basic, but that's the laksa bowl I'll forever think about."

Oh, Jamie, you're anything but basic! And I totally agree with you: Laksa is truly a culinary delight, a staple found across Southeast Asia, and as you said, the combo of spice, flavor, and texture is simply unbeatable!

P.S.: Thanks to Jamie for not only the inspiration but also testing the recipe. The first step of grinding the aromatics was her idea!

Neutral oil

2 garlic cloves, minced

1 teaspoon to 1 tablespoon (6 g) minced ginger

2 bird's eye chilies, chopped (optional because this dish is already spicy)

1 lemongrass, finely chopped

1 tablespoon (15 g) red or yellow curry paste

⅓ cup (76 g) store-bought laksa paste, adjust to taste as this is quite spicy

Dash of MSG (optional)

2 tablespoons (30 ml) fish sauce

1 teaspoon kosher salt

1 can (13.5 fl oz or 400 g) coconut milk

3 to 4 cups (705 to 940 ml) chicken or vegetable broth, depending on how thick you like your laksa broth

2 tablespoons (26 g) rock sugar or 1½ tablespoons (20 g) granulated sugar

12 fried tofu puffs, sliced in half (optional, though Jamie argues these are mandatory)

12 fish balls or 5.6 ounces (150 g) sliced fish cakes (optional)

8 medium to large shrimp, shelled and deveined (optional)

4 servings or 1 pound (454 g) mee tai bak noodles, vermicelli, or Hokkien egg noodles

FOR THE OPTIONAL TOPPINGS:

1 cup (50 g) bean sprouts (recommended)

4 soft- or hard-boiled eggs, halved lengthwise

Fresh cilantro or coriander

Fried shallots or fried garlic (recommended for the added crunch and texture)

FOR SERVING:

Lime or lemons, cut into wedges

Sambal on the side

1. Using a mortar and pestle or food processor, create a paste by grinding together the garlic, ginger, lemongrass, and optional chilies.

2. Heat 1 tablespoon (15 ml) neutral oil in a heavy saucepan or pot over medium-high heat. Once the oil is hot, add the paste and cook until aromatic, being cautious as lemongrass burns quickly. Stir in the curry paste and laksa paste, cooking until fragrant.

3. Stir in the MSG (if using), fish sauce, salt, coconut milk, broth, and sugar. Cook, stirring constantly, until bubbles form, about 2 minutes. Reduce the heat to low, cover, and let the mixture simmer for 10 minutes before adding the tofu, fish balls, fish cakes, and shrimp. Let the broth simmer until the optional ingredients are cooked through, such as when the shrimp turn pink, about 5 minutes.

4. Meanwhile, prepare the noodles according to the packaging instructions and drain them. Divide the noodles evenly among 4 bowls, and generously ladle the laksa broth over the noodles.

5. Garnish the noodles with the optional toppings, though it's highly recommended to include all of them for a full-flavored noodle soup. Serve with lime or lemon wedges and sambal on the side, and enjoy a little taste of Singapore at home!

NOTE: *There are many variations of laksa. For example, Brunei's curry laksa often includes bok choy, choy sum, long beans, or okra with a thick currylike broth. Asam laksa is tangy, with a tamarind-based broth. When asking the members of Subtle Asian Baking how they enjoyed their laksa, many recommended topping the noodle soup with sambal, an Indonesian chili paste. If you don't have lemongrass handy, substitute with lemon zest.*

PREP TIME	**15 MINUTES**
COOK TIME	**20 MINUTES**
YIELD	**4 SERVINGS**

Matcha Miso Ramen

One of my most cherished and unfor-gettable ramen experiences was trying the matcha ramen from Mensho Tokyo in Shinjuku. The broth was creamy and had a unique verdant hue, a color not often associated with ramen. This recipe is my attempt to re-create that memorable dish, bursting with flavor, umami, and comfort.

I am aware that traditional chashu, a common accompaniment to ramen, is made from marinated and braised skin-on pork belly that is rolled into a log and tied with twine, then sliced into round pieces. My version of chashu may not be entirely authentic, but it is quick, easy to make, and delicious—perfect for busy parents like me!

FOR THE MATCHA MISO PASTE:

¼ cup (62.5 g) white miso (white miso will make the green color more vibrant, but you can also use red if preferred)

2 tablespoons (32 g) creamy peanut butter, adjust to taste

1 tablespoon (15 ml) soy sauce, adjust to taste

3 tablespoons (45 ml) mirin

1 tablespoon (13 g) sugar

1 tablespoon (15 ml) rice wine vinegar

4 garlic cloves, minced

1 tablespoon (9 g) culinary-grade matcha, adjust to taste

FOR THE BROTH:

2 large onions, optional

6 cups (1.4 L) vegetable broth, chicken broth, or Homemade Awase Dashi (page 28)

FOR THE EASY "CHASHU":

2 garlic cloves, minced

8 thin and long slices of pork belly (about ⅛-inch [4 mm] thick)

Salt and pepper to taste

1 tablespoon (15 ml) soy sauce, adjust to taste

Sugar, for sprinkling

FOR THE NOODLES:

1 pound (454 g) ramen noodles

FOR THE OPTIONAL ADD-INS:

4 large soft-boiled eggs, halved

Soft or firm tofu, sliced and pan-fried until golden (optional)

FOR THE OPTIONAL TOPPINGS:

2 to 3 scallions, chopped

1 cup (50 g) bean sprouts, washed

2 tablespoons (30 g) fried shallots or garlic

Black or white sesame seeds

PREP TIME	15 MINUTES
COOK TIME	20 MINUTES
YIELD	4 SERVINGS

1. Make the matcha miso paste by whisking all the matcha miso paste ingredients in a bowl. Set aside.

2. Make the broth. If using onions for the broth, cut the onions in half and place them cut side down on a lined baking sheet. Roast in a preheated oven at 425°F (220°C) until golden brown and aromatic, about 25 to 30 minutes. Add the roasted onions to a heavy saucepan or pot along with the broth or dashi. Bring to a boil over high heat, then reduce to low and allow the soup to simmer. If not using onions, bring the broth to a boil just before serving the ramen.

3. Make the easy chashu. Preheat a wok or frying pan over medium-high heat. Add 1 teaspoon oil, followed by the minced garlic. Once the garlic is fragrant, add the pork belly slices. Season with salt and pepper, then drizzle with the soy sauce and sprinkle with sugar. Cook until the bottom is golden brown, about 1 to 2 minutes. Flip the pork belly, season again with salt and pepper, drizzle with soy sauce, and sprinkle with a bit more sugar. Cook until the other side is golden brown, another 1 to 2 minutes. Remove from heat. While it is still warm, optionally roll up each pork belly slice into a tight cylinder. Secure with a toothpick if needed, and set aside. Just be sure to remove the toothpicks before eating.

4. Cook the noodles according to the packaging instructions. Drain and rinse under cold water to halt the cooking process.

5. Assemble the ramen by adding 2 to 3 tablespoons of the matcha miso paste to each bowl and adjust to taste. Ladle approximately 1½ cups (350 ml) hot broth into each bowl. If the broth isn't hot enough, heat it again first. Divide the cooked noodles among the bowls, then add 2 slices (or rolls) of cooked pork belly and any optional add-ins. Finish with your chosen toppings and serve immediately.

TIP: *I recommend getting the ramen noodles found in the frozen noodle aisles of Asian supermarkets. Leftover matcha miso paste can be stored in an airtight container and frozen for up to 6 months.*

MAKE IT VEGAN: Substitute the chashu with pan-fried slices of portobello mushrooms, firm tofu, or eggplants. Use vegetable broth and vegan noodles, and omit the eggs. Purchase vegan ramen noodles.

ESSENTIAL SAUCES

"Woe to the cook whose sauce has no sting."
—Geoffrey Chaucer

When my editor Dan suggested I include an entire chapter on sauces, I hesitated. I initially wanted to reserve a chapter for fun drinks and mocktails! Being the flexible and easygoing and wonderful person I am, I conceded. I love sauces anyway and can drink them like soup. In fact, my sauces will make you sing.

Despite their versatility, sauces often play the role of underdogs or culinary wingmen when they deserve the spotlight. Are your boiled dumplings a bit bland? Dunk them in Kat's Everyday Dipping Sauce (page 168). You can even drizzle the sauce over cooked noodles for a quick meal. Searching for a versatile dipping sauce that doubles as a salad dressing? Whip up batches of Quick and Easy Nước Chấm (page 164), and you'll be amazed at how this zesty, sweet, and garlicky sauce pairs well with a wide variety of dishes, not just Vietnamese cuisine. For a little kitchen adventure, concoct your own signature blend of *Fire* Chili Crisp Oil (page 176). In this chapter, I've provided numerous ingredients for you to select and combine, crafting sauces that'll delightfully singe your taste buds and leave them craving more. So, what are you waiting for? It's time to get *saucy*!

Quick and Easy
Nước Chấm

Nước chấm is a dipping sauce that is sweet, sour, refreshing, and umami-savory all at once. You'll probably find it jarred or bottled in most Vietnamese households, living in the fridge. It comes out when the *gỏi cuốn* (spring rolls), *bún thịt nướng* (grilled pork noodle salad), *cơm tấm* (broken rice), or just about any other savory dish hit the sharing table.

The beauty of this sauce is how versatile and customizable it is. While lime juice is used for its crisp and refreshing flavor, Vietnamese restaurants often use vinegar instead to preserve the sauce. Try using both and add a little lime pulp!

RECIPE SPECS

2½ cups (587 ml) warm water

1 cup (200 g) white sugar

1 cup (235 ml) fish sauce

3 tablespoons (30 g) minced garlic

3 tablespoons (45 ml) lime or lemon juice (optional)

1 tablespoon (15 ml) white vinegar

½ teaspoon fresh chopped bird's eye chili (optional)

1 teaspoon lime pulp (optional)

1. In a mixing bowl, mix warm water and sugar together. Stir until all the sugar melts. Allow to cool down before mixing in the rest of the ingredients. Adjust to taste. Recipe testers Ingrid and Sabrina Koo prefer their sauce with more tang, so they added more lime juice. I like my nước chấm sweeter.

2. Transfer to dipping bowls and serve immediately.

3. Store leftover sauce in an airtight container in the refrigerator for up to a week (longer if you omit the fresh citrus juice and pulp). This sauce can also be frozen for up to 4 months.

TIP: If you don't need a lot of nước chấm (this recipe makes about 5 cups) and don't intend to store it for later use, scale down and use half the ingredients to make less sauce.

MAKE IT VEGAN: When making the sauce, use a vegan fish sauce or equal parts soy sauce and Maggi or other liquid aminos. If you have lemongrass handy, chop up a piece and add a little to the sauce!

PREP TIME	10 MINUTES
COOK TIME	10 MINUTES
YIELD	ABOUT 5 CUPS (1.2 L)

Kat's Everyday Dipping Sauce

This is my go-to everyday sauce for dipping dumplings like *xiao long bao* and *gyoza*, and for drizzling over cooked veggies, noodles, or savory pancakes like my Savory Green Onion and Kimchi Korean Pancakes (page 86). You'll see many of the ingredients I've listed are optional. My intention is for you to make this sauce your own. Test the flavors as you mix in the ingredients, as you know your palate best. Throw in some other spices, like cinnamon, if you'd like! I won't mind if you call it your everyday dipping sauce. I'd be honored if you do.

If you bottle and sell it, please offer me a cut. I'm a starving author, after all.

RECIPE SPECS

3 tablespoons (45 ml) soy sauce

1 tablespoon (15 ml) Chinkiang, black, or rice vinegar

1 teaspoon brown or granulated sugar

1 teaspoon sesame oil

¼ teaspoon sesame seeds, black or white (or mixed)

Pinch of five-spice (optional)

2 star anises (optional)

½ teaspoon chili flakes

1 tablespoon (10 g) minced garlic or shallots

1 stalk scallion, finely chopped

Splash of mirin (optional)

Dash of MSG (optional)

1. Make the dipping sauce. Combine all the ingredients for the dipping sauce in a bowl, stirring until the sugar dissolves. Remember to taste the sauce to adjust the flavor to your liking. You can use this sauce to enhance the taste of dishes like noodles, dim sum, bao, veggies, even mac and cheese, as well as stir-fried meats or savory pancakes.

2. Any leftover sauce can be stored in an airtight container in the refrigerator for up to a week.

NOTE: *For added flavor, you can toast the star anise, chili flakes, sesame seeds, garlic (or shallots), and scallions in a pan over medium-low heat for a few minutes (or in the oven at 350°F [180°C] for about 10 minutes). Cool before adding to the rest of the sauce.*

PREP TIME	**10 MINUTES**
COOK TIME	**50 TO 60 MINUTES**
INACTIVE TIME	**30 MINUTES**
YIELD	**ABOUT 2 SERVINGS**

Ah Ma's Simple Peanut Dipping Sauce

My mother loves making *gỏi cuốn* (Vietnamese spring rolls) at home. While her spring rolls have always been top-notch, at one point, the consistency and taste of the accompanying peanut sauce had room for improvement. I mentioned to her one afternoon sometime in the early 2000s, "Ah Ma adds glutinous rice to her sauce." Naturally, she doubted my suggestion (East Asian mothers, I tell you). We ended up calling Ah Ma, who confirmed she indeed used sweet glutinous rice in

her peanut sauce to both sweeten and thicken it. The triumphant "I told you so" look I shot at Mom was priceless.

Today, my mother rarely questions my elephantine memory, yet I still find her ability to drive me crazy unparalleled. Nonetheless, I love her dearly, and her spring rolls remain delicious, thanks to Ah Ma's perfected sauce. I believe this sauce can be used as a dip for various savory finger foods.

RECIPE SPECS

¾ cup (176 ml) water

½ cup (118 ml) hoisin sauce

1 tablespoon (15 ml) mirin, optional

3 tablespoons (48 g) crunchy or creamy peanut butter (adjust to taste)

2 tablespoons (30 ml) white or rice vinegar

2 tablespoons (20 g) glutinous rice flour

1 tablespoon (13 g) brown sugar

Chopped peanuts, optional

½ large onion, minced

1. In a blender, mix the water, hoisin sauce, optional mirin, peanut butter, vinegar, glutinous rice flour, sugar, and optional chopped peanuts until homogenous and smooth. Set aside.

2. Add the oil and minced onion to a saucepan and cook over medium heat until the onion becomes aromatic and translucent, a few minutes. If you'd like and have the time, you can continue cooking until the onion browns.

3. Add the onions to the blender with the sauce mixture and blend until smooth. Add everything to the saucepan.

3. Lower the heat to medium and pour in the blended mixture, stirring occasionally until the sauce thickens. Bear in mind that the sauce will further thicken once it cools. Personally, I prefer a thicker sauce, but a more fluid sauce is easier for dipping.

4. If the sauce seems too thick, gradually add water, a teaspoon at a time, and stir. If the sauce appears too thin, prepare a glutinous rice slurry by mixing 1 tablespoon (10 g) glutinous rice flour with 2 tablespoons (30 ml) water. Add a little of this slurry at a time and cook until the sauce reaches your desired consistency.

5. Once the sauce is ready, remove it from the heat and transfer it to a serving bowl. It can be used for dipping, or you can spoon it onto your spring rolls or other foods. I used to enjoy this sauce like a soup when I was a child, so no judgment here if you decide to do the same.

6. Store any leftover sauce in an airtight container in the refrigerator for up to 5 days, or freeze it for up to 3 months. To reheat, cook in a saucepan over medium heat or use the microwave.

NOTE: Sweet glutinous rice requires soaking and steaming, so while you can use it cooked and blended into the sauce, we will take a shortcut here and use glutinous rice flour. Ah Ma wouldn't mind this hack. A blender is needed for this recipe, or a large food processor. Immersion blenders work too.

TIP: I adore adding a hint of heat to this sauce, be it sriracha, any other chili paste, or *Fire* Chili Crisp Oil (page 176).

PREP TIME	5 MINUTES
COOK TIME	10 TO 15 MINUTES
YIELD	1 BOWL OF SAUCE

Ma Ma's Fish Sauce Butter

My friendship with Tres Truong sparked on TikTok, rapidly developing into a tight-knit online bond. When Tres shared her grandmother's fish sauce butter recipe and its accompanying story, I knew immediately that it deserved a spot in this book.

Tres's grandmother, Muoi Ngu, fondly known as Ma Ma, worked as a nanny for a French family in Ho Chi Minh City back when it was still Saigon. The French colonization of Vietnam led to the birth of many fusion dishes, like this fish sauce butter and the use of French baguettes in banh mi.

According to Tres, the children Ma Ma cared for were notoriously finicky eaters—a timeless tale indeed! They would only consume vegetables, bread, or rice if graced by Ma Ma's delicious umami-packed fish sauce butter. So, take a leaf out of Ma Ma's book: Add this sauce to any savory dish and watch your loved ones devour every bite.

RECIPE SPECS

4 tablespoons (55 g) butter, softened

2 tablespoons (30 ml) fish sauce

1 tablespoon (13 g) granulated sugar

3 garlic cloves, minced

1. Combine all the ingredients in a small saucepan and cook over medium-low heat until the garlic turns golden brown. Alternatively, place all the ingredients in a microwave-safe bowl and heat for about 90 seconds.

2. Use immediately by adding the sauce to dishes like smashed potatoes, chicken, or fish. Recipe testers Ingrid and Sabrina Koo (who felt this recipe was foolproof) suggest adding the sauce to freshly steamed rice or noodles, but using it sparingly as the flavor is quite intense.

3. Store any leftover fish sauce butter in an airtight container in the refrigerator for up to a week, or freeze for up to 3 months.

TIP: Tres enjoys using this sauce to elevate fried rice and baked potatoes. She recommends using Red Boat or Three Crabs fish sauce.

Tres Truong and her wonderful Ma Ma, Muoi Ngu

PREP TIME	10 MINUTES
COOK TIME	5 TO 10 MINUTES
YIELD	1 SMALL JAR OF FISH SAUCE BUTTER

MAKE IT VEGAN:
Swap butter for vegan butter and replace fish sauce with Maggi, liquid aminos, or soy sauce. Taste and adjust to suit your palate.

Tonkatsu Sauce

Tonkatsu sauce, a thick, rich, and subtly sweet condiment, hails from Japan and is traditionally served with tonkatsu. Its origins remain shrouded in mystery, with theories ranging from its invention in Yokohama in the early twentieth century to its creation by a food manufacturer in the 1930s. As Western flavors gained popularity in Asia, they were often melded into Japanese dishes, and tonkatsu sauce is a testament to this fusion. Regardless of its history, tonkatsu sauce enjoys widespread popularity, and I hope it soon finds a place among your favorites. Feel free to diversify its use beyond tonkatsu; it works wonders on vegetables, sandwiches, and grilled meats.

RECIPE SPECS

⅓ cup (106 g) ketchup

2 tablespoons (30 ml) Worcestershire sauce

2 tablespoons (30 ml) oyster sauce

2 tablespoons (26 g) brown sugar

2 tablespoons (30 ml) mirin

1 teaspoon dark soy sauce

½ teaspoon garlic powder or 1 teaspoon minced garlic

White or black sesame (optional)

1. Combine all ingredients in a small saucepan and adjust to taste as needed. Cook over medium heat, stirring occasionally, until the sauce reaches a simmer.

2. Reduce the heat to low and let the sauce simmer until it thickens slightly or reaches your desired consistency, a few minutes.

3. Remove the sauce from heat and allow it to cool to room temperature. If desired, serve topped with sesame seeds.

4. Store any leftover tonkatsu sauce in an airtight container in the refrigerator for up to 1 week.

MAKE IT VEGAN: Substitute Worcestershire sauce with balsamic vinegar and replace oyster sauce with a vegan alternative.

PREP TIME	5 TO 10 MINUTES
COOK TIME	10 MINUTES
YIELD	ABOUT ¾ CUP (176 ML)

Fiery Hot Mayo

This fiery hot mayo recipe is my take on spicy mayo, a condiment I instantly fell in love with. My first encounter was with a spicy sushi roll, where I initially mistook it for Thousand Island dressing. Its strikingly orange hue and creamy texture, packed with an unexpected kick, had me hooked. This fiery hot mayo is a must-have staple for any spicy food lover's fridge. The flavors from the hot sauce, vinegar/lime juice, and honey balance out the creaminess of the mayo, creating a spicy and tangy spread that's perfect for various dishes. So use it as a spread, dip, or drizzle on burgers, sandwiches, fries, poke bowls, and more. Or, thin it with water and oil to craft a lively salad dressing.

VEGETARIAN

RECIPE SPECS

- 1 cup (225 g) mayonnaise
- 1 to 2 tablespoons (15 to 30 ml) hot sauce of choice, like sriracha or gochujang
- Up to 1 tablespoon (15 ml) rice vinegar or lime juice, adjust to taste
- 2 garlic cloves, minced
- 1 tablespoon (20 g) honey
- ½ teaspoon paprika powder, to deepen the color

PREP TIME	5 TO 10 MINUTES
YIELD	ABOUT 1 CUP (225 G)

1. Mix all the ingredients in a small bowl and adjust the taste as necessary. You can add more mayonnaise if you want a thicker consistency. If you want it spicier, add more hot sauce.

2. Store the leftover condiment in an airtight container in the refrigerator for up to 2 weeks or longer. Some say mayonnaise can last in the refrigerator for more than a month.

MAKE IT VEGAN: Check the labels of your chosen hot sauce. Most sriracha, sambal, and gochujang are vegan-friendly. Omit the honey and substitute it with agave nectar or brown rice syrup for a touch of sweetness. Use plant-based mayonnaise.

Fire Chili Crisp Oil

Chili crisp oil is FIRE, as recipe tester Judy Shertzer's grandchildren would say. It's a versatile condiment that doesn't conform to a single recipe, so feel free to experiment and create your unique blend. That said, a delicious chili crisp oil generally includes garlic, black cardamom, and a form of glutamate like MSG. The oil can be peanut, rapeseed, or any other neutral oil. Jar up this deliciousness, gift one to a friend, and use it with all your noodles, veggies, dumplings, and finger foods, adding tingly excitement to any meal. Heck, try drizzling some over vanilla ice cream and thank me later.

2½ cups (588 ml) refined peanut, vegetable, or rapeseed oil

1½ cups (368 g) thinly sliced shallots (use a mandoline if you have one)

1 cup (136 g) thinly sliced garlic (use a mandoline if you have one, or chopped garlic is fine too)

About 1 cup (115 g) dried small chili peppers or gochugaru chili flakes, or a mix

2 tablespoons (12 g) chili powder (for the redness)

1 teaspoon paprika

1 teaspoon Sichuan peppercorns, adjust to taste—these will make your tongue numb and tingly (optional)

About ⅓ cup (50 g) chopped roasted peanuts (salted or unsalted)

2 tablespoons (19 g) toasted white sesame seeds

2 star anises

2 tablespoons (26 g) brown sugar

A pinch of cinnamon or five-spice

¼ teaspoon ground cumin (optional)

¼ teaspoon white or black pepper (optional)

¼ teaspoon ground black cardamom

2 to 3 bay leaves (optional)

1 teaspoon MSG (optional)

1 teaspoon mushroom powder, mushroom bouillon, or chicken bouillon

1 teaspoon kosher salt

1 tablespoon (15 ml) soy sauce

1 tablespoon (15 ml) sesame oil

PREP TIME	15 MINUTES
COOK TIME	10 MINUTES
YIELD	1 QUART

1. In a heavy saucepan, heat the oil over high until it reaches about 325°F (170°C). Add the shallots, lower the heat to medium-low, and stir until they turn golden brown and thoroughly crispy, which may take about 5 to 7 minutes. Remove the shallots with a strainer, keeping the oil in the saucepan. Set the shallots aside.

2. Add the garlic to the saucepan and cook over medium heat. Stir until the garlic becomes golden and crispy, about 3 to 5 minutes. Remove from heat and strain, reserving the oil. Set the garlic aside.

3. Grind the dried small chili peppers or gochugaru chili flakes until fine using a mortar and pestle or food processor. In a large heatproof bowl or container, combine the ground chili peppers or chili flakes with the rest of the ingredients and optional ingredients (up to and including the salt). At this point, you're not adding in the oil, shallots, garlic, soy sauce, and sesame oil yet.

4. Heat the reserved oil until it reaches 375°F (190°C). Carefully pour the hot oil over the bowl of chili mixture and spices, stirring to combine. Let it rest and cool for about 30 minutes. Once cooled, add the fried shallots and garlic. Mix in the soy sauce and sesame oil. Taste and adjust seasoning if necessary.

5. If you've used star anise and bay leaves, remove them before storing the chili crisp oil. Store the cooled oil in an airtight container in the refrigerator for up to 3 months, ensuring the shallots and garlic have been thoroughly fried to a crisp.

NOTE: *The "crisp" in chili crisp oil comes from the crispiness of fried shallots, garlic, nuts, sesame seeds, and chili flakes.*

TIP: *You can double or triple the ingredients here to make more chili oil for gifting.*

NOT-TOO-SWEET TREATS

"It's a common refrain in the Asian diaspora that calling a dessert 'not too sweet' is the peak form of praise."
—Bettina Makalintal

The media had crowned me the Queen and Doyenne of Asian Baking in 2022. While I graciously accepted this title and helped put the term "Asian baking" on the map back in 2020, it's important to remember that Asians have been baking and crafting desserts for thousands of years. The Chinese created mooncakes during the Tang Dynasty, and even earlier, around 3400 BCE, they used pottery tripods to steam buns made from millet. Across Asia, makeshift ovens made of brick, stone, or clay (like tandoors) were heated using charcoal or wood. Thanks to colonization and cultural exchange, Asians in Asia made Western-style desserts and cakes as early as the 1500s. So yes, Asian baking has been around for quite some time now.

Traditional Western baking often conjures images of frosting, icing, and extremely sweet treats, but Asian desserts tend to be more balanced and harmonious. This is one of the reasons why I love incorporating miso into my sweet creations, adding a bit of umami and salty flavor to desserts.

Take, for example, my Pork Floss Paper-Wrapped Sponge Cake (page 194). These cakes are soft, pillowy, and mildly sweet, balanced by savory pork floss. We don't usually imagine adding savory elements like scallions and pork to a cake, but you'll find many such combinations in Asian bakeries and recipes. Asian breads are known for their fluffy, soft texture and subtle sweetness. Don't miss my Queen of the Milk Bread recipe (page 180), which uses a versatile base dough to create Asian bakery favorites like my THW Char Siu Bao (page 56). You can also enjoy it on its own as a delicious sandwich bread or toast.

For a dessert that combines tradition with a contemporary twist, try my irresistible Melty Cheesecake Baos (page 182). Each fluffy steamed bun is filled with an oozy, creamy cheesecake center. If you're looking for something richer yet still easy to bake, give Kat's Heady Chinese Peanut Butter Cookies (page 184) a try. Finally, for a perfectly balanced dessert to share with loved ones and friends, my Sweet, but Not-Too-Sweet, Taro Sago (page 198) is a delightful dessert soup that proves that sometimes, less (sugar) is indeed more.

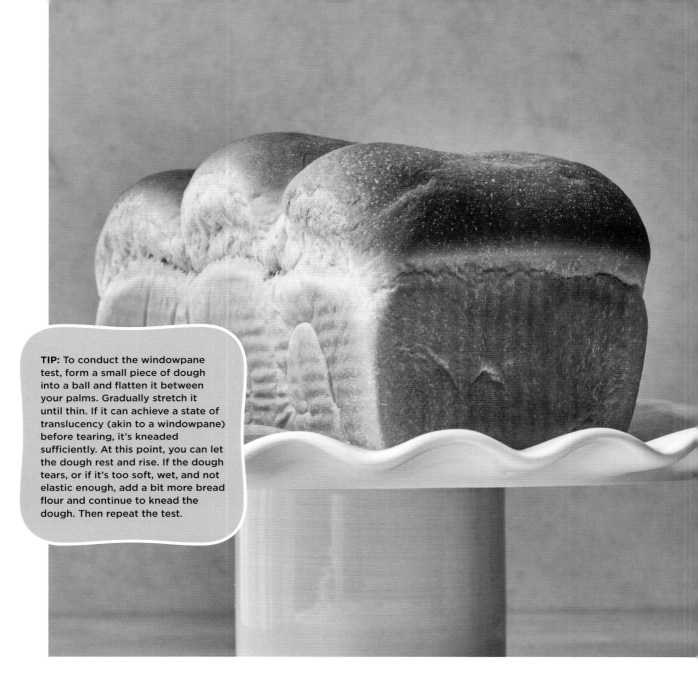

TIP: To conduct the windowpane test, form a small piece of dough into a ball and flatten it between your palms. Gradually stretch it until thin. If it can achieve a state of translucency (akin to a windowpane) before tearing, it's kneaded sufficiently. At this point, you can let the dough rest and rise. If the dough tears, or if it's too soft, wet, and not elastic enough, add a bit more bread flour and continue to knead the dough. Then repeat the test.

Queen of the Milk Bread

This bread, like me, is a queen. She's a staple found in Asian bakeries across the world. Use her dough to make delicious baked goodies like THW Char Siu Bao (page 56), cinnamon buns, dinner rolls, garlic knots, *shokupan*, and more.

Milk bread, like brioche, is sweet, soft, and creamy and enriched with butter and milk. Unlike brioche, milk bread is made with fewer eggs. Keep in mind, this bread will take a few hours to make, but you can cold-proof the dough, allowing the first rise to happen overnight in the refrigerator.

FOR THE TANGZHONG:

¼ cup (30 g) all-purpose flour

½ cup (118 ml) milk or plain plant-based milk

FOR THE DOUGH:

1 packet (7 to 8 g) active dry yeast

½ cup (118 ml) warm milk (about 110°F or 43°C) or plain plant-based milk

2⅓ cups (325 g) bread flour (plus more needed if the dough is too sticky, see step 2)

¼ cup plus 2 tablespoons (76 g) granulated sugar

½ teaspoon salt or 1 teaspoon miso

1 large egg or 50 g silken tofu

2 tablespoons (30 g) unsalted butter or vegan butter, melted

1 tablespoon (20 g) honey, agave syrup, or maple syrup

FOR THE EGG WASH:

1 egg, beaten, optional or coconut cream or plant-based creamer

1. Make the *tangzhong*. In a saucepan over low heat, whisk the flour and milk until no lumps remain. Once thickened to the consistency of smooth, sticky mashed potatoes, remove from heat, cover, and cool for 15 to 30 minutes. For a more traditional approach, some Asian bakeries will rest the tangzhong overnight. Alternatively, you can heat everything in the microwave in 30-second bursts until an extensible, sticky roux-dough forms.

2. Prepare the dough. Add the yeast and a dash of sugar to the warm milk. Let the mixture sit until it starts to foam and bubble, which should take a few minutes. In a stand mixer fitted with the dough hook attachment, combine all the dough ingredients: the yeast mixture, bread flour, sugar, salt or miso, egg or tofu, melted butter, and honey or syrup. Mix on low speed for about 5 minutes. Add the tangzhong and mix for an additional 5 minutes, until the dough becomes elastic and forms a smooth texture. This dough should be sticky, but you can knead in more flour (up to an extra ¾ to 1 cup [100 to 125 g], in increments) to make it more manageable. Perform the windowpane test (see the tip) to check the dough's readiness.

3. Flour your hands and shape the dough into a ball. Transfer it to a lightly greased bowl. Cover and proof until roughly doubled in size, about 60 minutes.

4. Butter a 9 x 5-inch (23 x 13-cm) loaf pan.

5. Deflate the dough and divide into 3 equal pieces.

6. With a floured rolling pin, roll each piece of dough into a long oval, about 10 inches (25 cm) long. Fold in the left and right sides of each dough toward the center to make a skinnier piece of dough. Starting from the bottom, roll each dough upward and away from you. Place the rolled dough, seam side down and side by side, in your prepared loaf pan.

7. Cover and proof for 60 minutes, until roughly doubled in size.

8. About 30 minutes before baking, preheat the oven to 350°F (180°C) with a rack in the center.

9. Brush the beaten egg or vegan wash evenly over the tops of each bun. Alternatively, you can skip the egg wash and dust the loaves with bread flour instead.

10. Bake for 30 to 35 minutes, until the tops are golden brown. Keep in mind that the exact baking time may vary depending on your oven.

11. Remove the bread from the oven. Enjoy immediately, as that's when it is the softest and fluffiest.

NOTE: *Tangzhong is a roux made by cooking water (or milk) and flour together. Functioning like a sponge, tangzhong helps bread absorb and retain more water during and after baking. This leads to irresistibly fluffy, pillowy, and flavorful milk bread that stays soft and tender for days.*

PREP TIME	**35 MINUTES**
COOK TIME	**30 TO 35 MINUTES**
INACTIVE TIME	**2 HOURS**
YIELD	**1 LOAF OF BREAD**

MAKE IT VEGAN: For the dough, use plant-based milk instead of milk. For the filling, use tofu or vegan cream cheese instead of cream cheese, and use vegan butter instead of butter.

Melty Cheesecake Baos

"Kat Lieu loves baos" is an understatement. As a child, I was never a fan of white bread, but I adored steamed buns, plain ones, filled ones; it didn't matter. I loved popping them into my mouth, enjoying their subtle sweetness and pillowy softness. I also appreciated how they're steamed—not baked in my childhood home's pot-and-pans-filled oven. Baos have always been and will always be special to me, and I'm delighted to present them here as a fun fusion dessert. These buns are fluffy and creamy, and when enjoyed hot, the melty cheesecake filling will ooze out like lava. Just watch out, as the filling could be super-hot.

FOR THE BAO DOUGH:

¾ cup plus 1 tablespoon (191 ml) milk, microwaved in 15-second bursts, until it reaches about 110°F (43°C)

1 teaspoon active dry yeast

2⅜ cups (300 g) all-purpose flour, sifted

Pinch of salt

¼ cup (50 g) granulated sugar

1 tablespoon (15 ml) vegetable or canola oil

1 to 2 teaspoons ube or green pandan extract (optional)

FOR THE CHEESECAKE FILLING:

7 ounces (200 g) cream cheese, softened

¼ cup (30 g) confectioners' sugar

1 tablespoon (14 g) unsalted butter, softened

1 tablespoon (8 g) cornstarch

1 teaspoon ube or green pandan extract (optional)

2 salted egg yolks, steamed for 15 minutes and mashed with a fork (optional)

FOR THE WASH:

Cream, milk, or plant-based milk for the milk wash

FOR THE OPTIONAL TOPPINGS:

White or black sesame seeds

Edible gold flakes

1. Line 2 bamboo or stainless steel steamers with perforated steamer parchment paper. (Alternatively, cut eight 4.5 x 4.5-inch [11 x 11-cm] parchment paper squares, 1 for each bao to sit on while steaming.)

2. Make the bao dough. In a large bowl, add the warmed milk, yeast, and a dash of sugar. Stir and set aside for a few minutes. If the mixture foams and bubbles, the yeast is alive. In a stand mixer fitted with the dough hook attachment (or by hand with a wooden spoon or chopsticks), tip in the dry ingredients, then slowly add the milk mixture, sugar, oil, and the optional ube or pandan extract. Mix on low speed just until a smooth and elastic dough forms, a few minutes. Do not overwork the dough. Shape into a ball, cover, and rest for 15 minutes.

3. Make the cheesecake filling. In a mixing bowl, combine the cream cheese, confectioners' sugar, butter, cornstarch, and optional extract. Fold in the optional salted egg yolk that has been steamed for 15 minutes and mashed with a fork. Divide into 8 even portions, either into 8 cups of a muffin tin or individually wrapped with plastic wrap. Freeze the filling until firm, at least 30 minutes.

4. Assemble the baos. Knead the dough for a few seconds. Divide the dough into 8 equal-size pieces. Working 1 at a time (cover the other ones with a damp kitchen towel), flatten into a disc with the edges thinner than the center. Shape each filling portion into a ball and place a ball of filling in the center of the disc. Fold the edges of the dough over the filling. Pinch the dough closed and roll the ball between your palms to round it out. Repeat with the remaining dough and filling.

5. Place the bao on the parchment paper or squares in the prepared steamers about 2 inches (5 cm) apart and 4 to a steamer. Cover and rest the bao until they grow about 1½ times their size, about 45 minutes.

6. Brush cream or milk wash evenly over the tops of the buns. Add the optional toppings, if desired, although edible gold flakes may be added after steaming. With 1 steamer stacked on top of the other and the top steamer covered, steam the buns for about 12 to 15 minutes over high heat. Periodically check the water level of the wok or pot and replenish with hot water as needed.

7. Remove from heat and serve piping hot. Steamed baos are best enjoyed fresh, but they can be stored in an airtight container in the refrigerator for up to 3 to 4 days. The best method to reheat the baos to retain their texture is to steam them again. Place the baos in a steamer over boiling water and steam for about 5 to 10 minutes, or until hot. Alternatively, reheat the baos in the microwave. Wrap the bun in a wet paper towel and microwave for about 20 to 30 seconds.

TIP: *Feel free, however, to change up the filling as you desire! Recipe tester Claire Fan recommends mixing cooked taro, red bean paste, or black sesame powder into the cheesecake filling. Also, please refer to the steamer setup instructions on page 15.*

PREP TIME	20 MINUTES
COOK TIME	ABOUT 30 MINUTES (COUNTING THE STEAMING OF THE SALTED EGG YOLKS)
INACTIVE TIME	1 HOUR
YIELD	8 BAOS

Kat's Heady Chinese Peanut Butter Cookies

According to legend, *hua sheng bing*, or Chinese peanut cookies, were first baked during the Qing Dynasty by skilled imperial pastry chefs who handcrafted these treats using ground peanuts, sugar, and flour. Nowadays, these cookies symbolize love and warmth and are enjoyed during Lunar New Year.

Since I had extra peanut butter at home, I cheated and used that instead of ground peanuts. For cookies that align more with the traditional texture, I suggest using nutty and crunchy peanut butter, but for creamier cookies, use smooth peanut butter. Either way, these cookies will be dreamy, melt-in-your-mouth, luxuriously heady, and warm. They're surprisingly easy to make and can even be shaped into different animal shapes. I hope you enjoy them with your family and friends year-round and not just during Lunar New Year.

P.S.: These cookies are delicious with a hot cup of tea, like oolong, black, or jasmine.

RECIPE SPECS

1 tablespoon (14 g) unsalted butter, softened

¼ cup (50 g) granulated sugar

3 tablespoons (45 g) brown sugar

½ to 1 tablespoon miso (red or white) or substitute with ¼ to ⅓ teaspoon kosher salt, adjust to taste

1 cup (250 g) crunchy or smooth natural (non-hydrogenated) peanut butter

¾ cup (100 g) all-purpose flour

1 teaspoon baking powder

A pinch of baking soda

12 to 15 shelled peanuts, salted or unsalted

1 egg yolk, beaten for egg wash

1. In a stand mixer fitted with the paddle attachment, add the butter, granulated sugar, and brown sugar and mix until fluffy, a few minutes. Scrape the sides of the bowl as needed with a spatula.

2. Add the miso (if using) and peanut butter and mix for a few seconds before adding the flour, baking powder, and baking soda. Mix until a dough forms. Again, scrape the sides of the bowl as needed. If the dough feels too dry and crumbly, add a little more peanut butter, about up to 1 to 2 tablespoons (16 to 32 g). Cover the dough with plastic wrap or transfer to an airtight container and refrigerate for at least 30 minutes to 1 hour. This cookie dough can also be stored in the refrigerator for a few days, or up to 5 months in the freezer.

3. About 20 to 30 minutes before baking, preheat the oven to 350°F (180°C) with a rack in the center. Line a baking sheet with parchment paper or a silicon mat.

4. I like these cookies big and chonky, like ping-pong balls, about 1.3 ounces (36 g) each or more than a heaping tablespoon. You'll have about 12 to 15 portions; roll each into a ball between your palms. You may need to compact and squeeze the ball together a bit to keep its shape.

5. Press a whole peanut into the center of each cookie ball. Transfer the cookie balls to the baking sheet, giving each space. While they won't expand much while baking, they will need consistent airflow to bake nicely. Brush all the tops with the egg wash.

6. Bake until the tops shine and the edges are browner, about 16 to 18 minutes.

7. Allow the cookies to cool on the baking sheet and enjoy them warm.

8. Store leftover cookies in an airtight container at room temperature for up to 1 week. If you've frozen any, they can be defrosted at room temperature for a few hours and refreshed in the oven at 350°F (180°C) for a few minutes to restore their original texture.

NOTE: *While I love bigger cookies, the portions I listed here may feel too filling for some, so you can divide the dough into smaller balls, about 15 grams each, and make about 24 to 30 cookies instead of 12. You'll need more peanuts and bake for less time, so plan accordingly.*

MAKE IT VEGAN: *Substitute butter with vegan butter and substitute the egg wash with any plant-based milk or melted vegan butter. A touch of agave nectar or maple syrup mixed with plant-based milk gives the cookies a nice sheen.*

PREP TIME	**15 MINUTES**
COOK TIME	**18 MINUTES**
YIELD	**12 TO 15 COOKIES**

DIY Halo-Halo Adventure

I had to marry Jake after he introduced me to delicious Filipino food like halo-halo, a refreshing and colorful dessert that means "mix-mix" or "mixed" in Tagalog. (Whether it means a mix of ingredients or you're supposed to mix everything, I'm not 100% sure!) I believe there's no wrong or one way to make halo-halo, making this dessert a fun and highly customizable

adventure. I did, however, consult my mother-in-law, Lilanie So Young, for her help to compile a list of some of the common mix-ins in the ingredients section. Feel free to change things up. Add boba if you'd like. The one ingredient you must have in halo-halo is shaved ice, often layered with evaporated and sweetened condensed milk.

2 to 4 cups (280 to 560 g) shaved ice

¼ to ½ cup (59 to 118 ml) evaporated milk or coconut milk

Sweetened condensed milk, or pandan condensed milk, to taste

Ice cream: ube, coconut, cheese, or any flavor of your choice

Roasted peanuts, chopped, to top the halo-halo (optional)

FOR THE OPTIONAL MIX-INS (PICK ANY 4 TO 5 FROM THE FOLLOWING LIST; PREPARE ABOUT ¼ TO ⅓ CUP [WEIGHT VARIES] OF EACH):

Any cooked sweet beans (red, kidney, or mung)

Toasted coconut strips

***Nata de coco* (coconut gel)**

***Kaong* (palm fruit)**

Leche flan

Jackfruit

Cooked sago or boba

Sliced mangoes

Sliced bananas or plantains

Canned corn

Crunchy cereal, like cornflakes

Shredded coconut flakes

Sweet potato, taro, or ube

1. In 4 tall glasses or glass bowls, layer the shaved ice, evaporated milk, and your chosen 4 to 5 ingredients in any order you prefer.

2. Top your halo-halo with a scoop of ice cream and drizzle with condensed milk.

3. Serve immediately and enjoy the mix-and-match adventure that is halo-halo!

NOTE: *It's up to you whether you want to enjoy halo-halo parfait-style or in a large bowl. Jake prefers the latter. Either way, have fun layering the ingredients and choose contrasting textures. Halo-halo almost always melts before you finish it, transforming into a sweet drink, perfect during the summertime, or for Jake and me, for any occasion.*

And don't worry: While I'm still low-hanging fruit and can be won over by good food, my marriage to Jake has been and continues to be adventurous and sweet, just like halo-halo.

PREP TIME	**10 TO 15 MINUTES**
YIELD	**4 SERVINGS**

Philip's Favorite Fried Sesame Balls

My neighbor Mindy often brings us these delightful fried sesame balls, knowing how much Philip enjoys them. As highly customizable gluten-free snacks (which can even be made vegan), these sesame balls, traditionally known as *jian dui* in China and *onde-onde* in Indonesia, can be filled with just about anything. Traditionally, they're filled with sweetened lotus paste, but they're so versatile that they pair well with either sweet or savory fillings. I couldn't pick just one favorite, so I've included a few variations, including my personal favorite—a melty cheesecake filling.

RECIPE SPECS

FOR THE SESAME BALL DOUGH:

2¼ cups (356 g) glutinous rice flour

½ teaspoon miso or pinch of salt

1 cup (235 ml) water

⅓ cup (67 g) granulated sugar plus 1 tablespoon (13 g) brown sugar

Neutral oil for frying

A small bowl of cold water

½ cup (72 g) sesame seeds, placed in a bowl (you may end up needing more!)

FOR THE FILLING:

About 225 grams filling of choice (it could be peanut butter, black sesame paste, *ube halaya* [purple yam jam], anko paste, or savory dumpling filling)

OR

FOR THE CHEESECAKE FILLING, BLEND OR MIX THESE INGREDIENTS TOGETHER UNTIL SMOOTH:

100 g steamed or cooked taro

1 teaspoon ube extract

½ brick or 4 ounces (113 g) cream cheese, softened

¼ cup (50 g) sugar

1 teaspoon miso

3 tablespoons (45 ml) heavy cream

1. Make the sesame ball dough. Add the glutinous rice flour and miso or salt to a large bowl. Make a well in the center of the flour. In a saucepan, bring the water to a boil, add in the sugar, stirring until all the sugar dissolves into a simple syrup. Pour the simple syrup into the well and, using a spatula, combine until a dough forms. Be careful: This dough is very hot! You can also use a stand mixer fitted with a paddle attachment for this step. Once the dough is ready, divide it in half. Microwave 1 portion of the dough in 30-second bursts until it turns translucent and shiny. Once cool enough to handle, knead both dough portions together on a lightly floured surface for about 5 minutes.

2. Divide the combined dough into about 11 even pieces, each about 2 inches (5 cm) in diameter and weighing 60 grams. If the dough is too sticky (it should be sticky but workable), dust it with a bit more glutinous rice flour, or rub neutral oil over your hands. Roll each piece into a ball and flatten it into a disc, with edges slightly thinner than the center.

3. Place about 1 heaping teaspoon (20 g) of your chosen filling in the center of each disc. If possible, shape the filling into a ball first. Fold the dough edges over the filling, pinch the seams together, and roll into a smooth ball.

4. Quickly dip each ball into the bowl of cold water, then roll it in the sesame seeds to coat thoroughly.

5. In a saucepan or pot, add enough neutral oil to fully submerge the sesame balls during frying. Heat the oil to 350°F (180°C) over medium to medium-high heat.

6. Reduce the heat to medium-low. Fry the sesame balls, in batches of about 4 at a time, until they turn golden brown and float to the top. They should feel hard, not soft or squishy. Use a slotted spoon or strainer to remove the balls and transfer them to a plate lined with oil-absorbing paper or a wire rack. These tend to become oily once cooled, so serve while they're still hot or warm.

NOTE: *This recipe makes 11 large sesame balls. Feel free to make yours smaller by dividing the dough into about 16 even portions, using less filling for each.*

TIP: *Refer to page 41 of* Modern Asian Baking at Home *for my anko (red bean) paste recipe. For the fillings, like my cheesecake one, I recommend freezing for 20 to 30 minutes to make it easier to handle.*

PREP TIME	30 MINUTES
COOK TIME	20 MINUTES
YIELD	ABOUT 11 LARGE SESAME BALLS

Gochujang Chocolate Mochi Cake

Chocolate lovers, this is the cake for you. It's not too sweet, has a fun chew, and will undoubtedly be a stunner at any potluck. If you love to spice things up, drop a heaping tablespoon of gochujang into the batter. Then decorate the cake however way you'd like, because you can't really go wrong with a beautiful chocolate canvas like this. Enjoy the cake hot, right out of the oven, or give it a day for the mochi to cure. The cake will be chewier then.

2 large eggs (about 3.5 ounces or 100 g)

1 cup (200 g) granulated sugar

¼ cup (59 ml) sweetened condensed milk

1 teaspoon miso or ¼ teaspoon kosher salt

Up to 1 heaping tablespoon (17 g) gochujang, adjust to taste

1 cup (235 ml) milk

2 tablespoons (28 g) unsalted butter, melted

1 teaspoon baking powder

About 1⅛ cups (296 g) glutinous rice flour

1 tablespoon (8 g) cornstarch

2 tablespoons (14 g) Dutch-processed cocoa powder, sifted

⅓ cup (60 g) finely chopped or flaked semi-sweet chocolate

FOR THE OPTIONAL TOPPINGS:

Confectioners' sugar

Cocoa powder

Paprika

Sliced strawberries

Sweetened condensed milk

Edible gold flakes

1. Preheat the oven to 350°F (180°C) with a rack in the center. Generously grease with cooking spray or line an 8-inch (20-cm) round cake pan with parchment paper (including the rim).

2. In a large bowl or a stand mixer fitted with the paddle attachment, whisk together the eggs, sugar, condensed milk, miso (or salt), and gochujang. Once the mixture is fluffy, whisk in the milk and melted butter until combined. Sift in the dry ingredients: baking powder, glutinous rice flour, cornstarch, and cocoa powder. Mix until well combined.

3. Pour the mochi batter into the prepared pan. Spread on the chocolate chips or chopped chocolate, evenly distributing them around the top of the cake. Bake until an inserted toothpick or bamboo skewer comes out clean and the top is semi-cracked, with brownielike crust, about 50 minutes.

4. Remove from the oven and let the cake cool in the pan itself or take it out to cool on a wire rack. If you prefer cakes sweeter, drizzle with a liquid sweetener of choice. Decorating with sliced fruits, like strawberries, gives the cake a beautiful pop of color, and if you love edible gold flakes like I do, add them! Dust with confectioners' sugar and/or cocoa powder, if desired, slice, and serve.

5. Store leftover cake in an airtight container. It should still be good and chewy the next day.

NOTE: *If you prefer a nonspicy chocolate cake, simply leave out the gochujang. Please note that most gochujang isn't gluten-free, so therefore including it makes this cake not gluten-free.*

MAKE IT VEGAN: Substitute the eggs with 3.5 ounces (100 g) silken tofu, the condensed milk with vegan condensed milk (available at health food stores or online) or agave syrup, the milk with water or plain plant-based milk, the butter with vegan butter or neutral oil, and use vegan-friendly chocolate chips.

PREP TIME	**15 MINUTES**
COOK TIME	**50 MINUTES**
YIELD	**ONE 8-INCH (20-CM) CAKE**

Hong Kong Bubble Waffles (Gai Daan Jai / 鷄蛋仔)

Developing this recipe transported me back to the 1990s, when my mother would buy my sister and me about twenty pieces of *gai daan jai* in a small paper baggy for about $2 from an NYC Chinatown street vendor stationed on the corner of Bowery and Pell. Mom simultaneously fed our sweet teeth and her nostalgia for Hong Kong, her home city. Plus, she got to support a fellow Hong Konger.

Hong Kong is home to iconic treats and street food like egg tarts and bubble waffles. Around the 1950s, Hong Kong street vendors needed a way to repurpose broken eggs and ingenuously created bubble waffles. These days, you can find bubble waffles in boba shops worldwide. Some are plain or decorated with toppings, and others are stuffed with sweet or savory fillings. Any way you make a bubble waffle, it'll surely be a beloved and tasty treat for you and your loved ones.

Recipe tester Susan Louangsaysongkham can attest to this: "My toddler was a HUGE fan of these bubble waffles! She kept stomping back and crying for more!"

FOR THE WAFFLE BATTER:

2¼ cups (280 g) cake flour, sifted

2 teaspoons baking powder

2 tablespoons (32 g) custard powder, milk powder, or coconut powder

⅜ cup (60 g) tapioca starch or sweet glutinous rice flour

1½ cups (240 g) granulated sugar (Susan recommends adding a little more sugar if you have a sweet tooth)

1 egg, optional

1⅖ cups (329 ml) water or any milk

¼ cup (60 ml) canola or vegetable oil

2 teaspoons vanilla extract (optional)

1 teaspoon miso, red or white or a dash of kosher salt

FOR THE OPTIONAL TOPPINGS:

Whipped cream

Cut fruits or berries

Syrup or jams

1. Hand mix or blend all the waffle batter ingredients in a blender. Rest the batter for at least an hour in the refrigerator. This batter can be stored in an airtight container for up to 5 days in the refrigerator.

2. Preheat a cast-iron bubble waffle pan or an electric bubble waffle maker. If using a cast-iron pan, use low heat.

3. Lightly grease the pan or waffle maker. (Note that when the waffle maker is not greased or very lightly greased, the waffles come out shinier and smoother.) Use a ladle and fill the waffle pan about two-thirds full to prevent a mess when excess batter spills out. Usually, depending on your waffle maker, this is about ½ to ¾ cup (118 to 176 ml) of batter.

4. Close the lid, swirl the pan gently, and do a 180 flip. Follow the instructions of the electric bubble waffle maker. For a cast-iron bubble waffle pan, cook over low heat until golden brown on the bottom, about 90 seconds. Flip again and cook the second side until golden brown, 60 to 90 seconds.

5. Remove the bubble waffle and transfer to a wire rack. Repeat with the remaining batter.

6. Bubble waffles are served hot or warm, with or without optional toppings. Go ahead and pop them with your fingers, and enjoy!

NOTE: *For gluten-free bubble waffle and mochi waffle recipes, visit modernasianbaking.com.*

TIP: *If you'd like to change the flavor of the waffle, feel free to add food extracts or food powders, like matcha or cocoa powder, as desired. Mix-ins, such as cooked boba, chocolate chips, nuts, or even bacon bits and shredded cheese, open up a realm of possibilities. Pour a little batter into the pan or waffle maker, top with some mix-ins of choice, and top with more batter.*

PREP TIME	5 MINUTES
COOK TIME	5 MINUTES
INACTIVE TIME	30 MINUTES
YIELD	APPROXIMATELY 6 BUBBLE WAFFLES, DEPENDING ON THE SIZE OF YOUR WAFFLE MAKER

Pork Floss Paper-Wrapped Sponge Cakes

Paper-wrapped sponge cakes are one of my favorite Chinese bakery staples. As a child, having just one of these sponge cakes was never enough, especially the ones from Kam Hing in NYC Chinatown. They're also perfect for my palate being not too sweet. Imagine if marshmallows and clouds had babies; those babies would be these sponge cakes. Traditionally, these sponge cakes are egg- and vanilla-flavored when you find them in Hong Kong or diaspora Chinatown bakeries. I made them sweet and savory here with the addition of pork floss and furikake.

FOR THE YOLK BATTER:

2½ tablespoons (37 ml) neutral oil, like canola or vegetable

⅝ cup (75 g) cake flour

4 large egg yolks

½ teaspoon baking powder

1 teaspoon miso or ¼ teaspoon salt

2 tablespoons plus 1 teaspoon (30 g) granulated sugar

2½ tablespoons (37 ml) milk or plant-based milk

FOR THE FIRM PEAKS MERINGUE:

4 large egg whites

½ teaspoon cream of tartar or ½ teaspoon lemon juice or white vinegar

2 tablespoons plus 1 teaspoon (30 g) granulated sugar

FOR THE PORK FLOSS TOPPING:

¼ cup (60 g) mayonnaise or Kewpie mayo

6 tablespoons (28 g) store-bought pork floss

FOR THE OPTIONAL TOPPINGS:

Sesame seeds

Furikake

Cooked salted egg yolk, crushed

Chopped scallions

Coconut flakes

PREP TIME	15 MINUTES
COOK TIME	20 TO 22 MINUTES
YIELD	6 TALL SPONGE CAKES

1. Preheat the oven to 325°F (170°C) with a rack in the center. Line 6 tall muffin tins or 6 cups of a jumbo muffin pan with liners and set aside.

2. Make the yolk batter. In a large heatproof bowl, microwave the oil in 20-second bursts until it reaches about 176°F (80°C). (Alternatively, heat the oil in a saucepan.) Add the cake flour and whisk until combined, like a runny paste. Beat in the egg yolks, baking powder, miso, and sugar and whisk until combined. It will probably look gritty at this point, like something you want to toss away, but don't! Mix in the milk or plant-based milk and whisk until smooth. (See, it worked out!) Set aside.

3. Make the firm peaks meringue. In a stand mixer fitted with the whisk attachment, beat the egg whites until foamy, then add the cream of tartar (or lemon juice or white vinegar). Beat for another minute, until whiter, then gradually add the sugar, about 10 g at a time. Beat until firm peaks form. (When you flip the whisk upside down, the peak, while more distinct than soft peaks, will still droop and curl back on itself, like a defined bird's beak.)

4. Mix the final batter. Add one-fourth of the meringue to the yolk batter. Gently whisk until incorporated. Add another fourth of the meringue to the yolk batter and whisk until incorporated. Then add all the yolk batter mixture into the bowl with the remaining meringue. Use a flexible spatula to gently fold the meringue into the batter, until homogenous, thick, and creamy. There should be no white streaks remaining in the batter. If stubborn lumps of meringue remain, use a whisk to gently mix the final batter, which should resemble a thick custard milkshake. Transfer the batter evenly into the lined muffin tins or cups; each should be about three-quarters full.

5. Bake until the tops are golden brown, 20 to 22 minutes. These cakes should not crack, but some cracks on the surface are to be expected. Remove from the oven and cool on a wire rack.

6. While you can enjoy these sponge cakes plain, I like to spread or drizzle about 1 teaspoon of mayonnaise over the top of each, then top evenly with a thin layer of pork floss. Feel free to also sprinkle on sesame seeds, furikake, and crushed salted egg yolk if desired. If you want the sponge cakes to be sweeter, use sweetened condensed milk instead of mayonnaise. Enjoy!

TIP: You can, of course, skip adding the pork floss. These sponge cakes can still be enjoyed without any toppings. For a change in color and flavor, you could try mixing about 1 to 2 teaspoons of ube or pandan extract into the batter. For added delightfulness, add a piece of mochi, taro, or ube paste or pork floss to the middle of the batter before baking. If you add cooked salted egg yolk crumbles to the pork floss, you'll create something similar to *bánh bông lan trứng muối*, a Vietnamese pork floss cake.

TIP: First divide 4 large eggs by adding the egg whites to a large mixing bowl or the bowl of a stand mixer and adding the yolks to another mixing bowl.

Pandan Tres Leches with Kaya Drizzle

Tres leches (or three-milk cake) is Nicaragua's national dessert and one of my all-time favorite treats. I've transformed this classic dish, poking and then soaking an airy pandan sponge cake with a pandan tres leches mixture. This beauty also has a hint of umami, thanks to the miso. Lovely and light, yet decadent and unforgettable, my pandan tres leches deserves to be this book's pièce de résistance dessert, *n'est pas*? (Fun albeit sad fact: In my youth, I studied French for more than a decade and this is the best I can do. *Quel dommage!*)

FOR THE YOLK BATTER:

4 large egg yolks

2 tablespoons plus 1 teaspoon (30 g) granulated sugar

½ cup plus 1½ tablespoons (140 ml) full-fat coconut milk

1 teaspoon miso

1 to 2 teaspoons pandan extract

1 cup (120 g) cake flour, sifted

1 teaspoon baking powder

FOR THE FIRM-TO-STIFF PEAKS MERINGUE:

4 large egg whites

¼ teaspoon cream of tartar or ¼ teaspoon lemon juice or white vinegar

½ cup (60 g) confectioners' sugar

FOR THE TRES LECHES (THREE MILKS) BATH:

½ cup (118 ml) evaporated milk

½ cup (118 ml) whole milk

⅓ cup (78 ml) condensed milk

1 teaspoon miso

1 teaspoon pandan extract (with color)

1 teaspoon coconut extract (optional)

FOR THE WHIPPED CREAM:

1 cup (235 ml) heavy cream

2 tablespoons (15 g) confectioners' sugar

FOR THE OPTIONAL KAYA DRIZZLE:

2 tablespoons (40 g) store-bought *kaya* (Malaysian coconut jam) mixed with 1 to 2 teaspoons hot water (you want a syrupy consistency, so if it's too runny, add more kaya)

FOR THE OPTIONAL GARNISHING:

Edible gold flakes

Berries of choice

Coconut shreds or flakes

Sea salt flakes

PREP TIME	**30 MINUTES**
COOK TIME	**20 TO 25 MINUTES**
INACTIVE TIME	**30 MINUTES**
YIELD	**9 SLICES OF PANDAN TRES LECHES CAKE**

1. Preheat the oven to 325°F (160°C) and position a rack in the center. Grease an 8 x 8-inch (20 x 20-cm) baking pan with pan spray or butter.

2. Prepare the yolk batter. In a mixing bowl, combine the yolks and sugar until smooth, creamy, and lighter in color, a few minutes. (Alternatively, use a stand mixer fitted with a paddle attachment, but note that you'll be using the stand mixer to beat egg whites later.) Stir in the coconut milk, miso, and pandan extract until well-blended. Sift in the cake flour and baking powder, mixing until combined. Set aside.

3. Create the firm-to-stiff peaks meringue. In a stand mixer fitted with the whisk attachment, beat the egg whites until foamy. Add the cream of tartar (or lemon juice or vinegar) and beat for another minute until the mixture turns whiter. Gradually add the sugar, a few teaspoons at a time, and continue beating until firm peaks form. (When you lift the whisk, the peak should droop and curl back on itself like a well-defined bird's beak.)

4. Make the final batter. Add one-fourth of the meringue to the yolk batter and gently whisk until incorporated. Repeat with another fourth of the meringue. Next, pour the entire yolk batter mixture into the bowl containing the remaining meringue. Gently fold the meringue into the batter using a flexible spatula until the mixture is uniform, thick, and creamy, with no white streaks remaining. If any stubborn meringue lumps persist, gently whisk the batter without overmixing.

5. Pour the batter into the prepared pan. Tap the pan against a counter 3 times to remove air bubbles and break any remaining bubbles with a whisk or chopstick. Bake until a toothpick or skewer inserted in the center comes out clean, 20 to 25 minutes. Depending on your oven and how it heats, the cake may require up to 35 minutes to bake.

6. Remove the cake from the oven and let it cool. Poke holes all over the cake, from top to bottom, using chopsticks.

7. Prepare the milk bath by combining all the milk bath ingredients and mixing well. Drizzle the milk bath evenly over the cooled cake.

8. Refrigerate the cake for at least 2 hours to allow it to absorb the milk bath. To serve, make the whipped cream by whipping the heavy cream in a stand mixer fitted with the whisk attachment until slightly thickened. Add the sugar and beat until stiff peaks form. (Overbeating will curdle the whipped cream.) Spread the whipped cream over the cake with an offset spatula, leveling and smoothing the surface. Optionally, reserve some whipped cream to pipe designs onto the cake.

9. Garnish the cake with optional toppings such as berries and coconut shreds and drizzle with optional kaya drizzle. Cut the cake into 9 equal pieces, serve, and enjoy with hot tea!

Sweet, but Not-Too-Sweet, Taro Sago

At almost every Cantonese banquet or dinner out I've been to, from New York to Seattle, Montreal to Hong Kong, the dessert to end on a not-too-sweet note is *burbur cha cha* (**摩摩喳喳**), originating from Malaysia. Similarly, the Philippines has *ginataan bilo bilo*, usually made with jackfruit and plantains. (It's one of Jake's favorite desserts!)

Creamy, heartwarming, and not-too-sweet (the ultimate compliment from East Asian aunties and mothers for desserts), it's the Goldilocks of sweets that can be eaten hot or cold; it's my all-time favorite dish to end any meal with friends and loved ones.

VEGAN & GLUTEN-FREE

FOR THE OPTIONAL MOCHI BALLS:

1 cup (158 g) glutinous rice flour

½ cup (118 ml) water

¼ cup (30 g) confectioners' sugar

Pinch of salt

Food coloring gel (optional)

FOR THE SAGO:

About ¼ cup (45 g) uncooked sago pearls

FOR THE SWEET SOUP:

14 ounces (400 g) taro, diced into ½-inch (1-cm) cubes, and steamed or boiled until softened, 15 to 20 minutes

1 can (13.5 oz or 400 ml) coconut milk

1 cup (235 ml) water

¾ to 1 cup (150 to 200 g) sugar, adjust to taste

1 teaspoon ginger juice (optional)

1 teaspoon vanilla extract

1 tablespoon (17 g) miso

A drop of purple food coloring gel or ube extract, for lavender coloring

FOR THE OPTIONAL TOPPINGS:

Cornflakes or other crunchy cereal of choice

Toasted coconut shreds or flakes

Edible lavender for decoration and aroma

Edible gold flakes for decoration

Liquid sweetener for drizzling (adjust to taste)

1. Make the optional mochi balls. Mix the glutinous rice flour, water, sugar, and salt all together in a bowl until a soft, playdoughlike dough forms. If the dough is too dry and crumbly, add a bit of water, a teaspoon at a time, until the desired consistency is reached. If you want 3 different colors of mochi balls, divide the dough into 3 portions and add drops of different food coloring gel to each portion, kneading until the color is evenly distributed. Shape the dough into ¼- to ½-inch (6 mm to 1 cm) rounds, or any other creative shape you desire. To cook the mochi balls, add them to a saucepan or pot of boiling water and cook over medium heat until the balls float up, a few minutes. Strain the balls and set them aside.

2. Cook the sago. In a large pot, bring 5 cups (1.2 L) water to a rolling boil. Add the sago and cook over medium heat until the sago is completely translucent, 15 to 20 minutes. The sago is not ready for consumption if the center is still white and opaque. Drain the sago and run it under cold water for a few seconds. Set it aside.

3. Make the sweet soup. Blend half of the taro with the coconut milk, water, miso, food coloring gel, and vanilla extract until the mixture is smooth. There's no need to strain this mixture; transfer to a pot and cook over medium heat. Add in the remaining taro, cooked sago, sugar, and mochi balls (if you made them), and continuously stir until the sweet soup simmers.

4. Remove the pot from heat. Optionally, add toppings of your choice. Serve hot, or chill in the refrigerator for a few hours to serve cold. Enjoy with loved ones, after a warm meal, and may good food forever bless your table, dear friend.

TIP: *Start with ¾ cup (150 g) sugar, and then taste the mixture before it begins to simmer. Add more sugar if desired, up to 1 cup total, or more if you have a sweet tooth.*

Until next time! 🤍

PREP TIME	30 MINUTES
COOK TIME	30 MINUTES
YIELD	4 TO 6 SERVINGS

Jake and Philip building our outdoor kitchen

Acknowledgments

To my eternal cheerleaders, my husband Jake, my dear son Philip, and my mom, Winnie. My canine companion, Panda, who sits behind me every day as I write, my doggy shadow. To my snail, Escargot, who has survived more than two years now after I stepped on them and broke their shell. Who would have thought a snail could teach a human so much about resiliency and never giving up?

To my amazing recipe testers: Without this amazing team of recipe testers, I could not have completed this book. So thank you to these amazing humans and the loved ones who served as their guinea pigs:

Jamie Aragonez

Mindy Cheung (and her husband)

Claire Fan

Lingjie He

Sharon Hsu (and Eddie Hsu)

Shannon Kish

Ingrid and Sabrina Koo

Susan Louangsaysongkham and family

R.J. Moorhouse

Kathleen Ng

Chi Nguyen

Jonni Scott

Judy Shertzer and her grandchildren

Jo Ann Wong

To my amazing photography team, Michelle K. Min, Selina S. Lee, Lizzie Oh, and team!!!!! YOU QUEENS ROCK!

To my family at Subtle Asian Baking 🤍

Thank you once again to my amazing team at Quarto US/Harvard Common Press: my editor, Dan Rosenberg, a lovable grump who is okay with me living on the streets (inside joke); my beautiful and elegant art director, Anne Re, who is probably tired of me asking for gold foil on my book covers; my managing editor, Meredith Quinn; my copy editor, Stephanie Cohen; my proofreader, Kelly Messier; editorial intern, Sydney Leclerc; my jolly, tireless marketing manager, Todd Conly; my sales rep, Monica Baggio; and the big bosses, Erik Gilg, publisher, and Giuliana Caranante, publicity and marketing director.

Finally, a shout-out to Jonathan Simcosky: Without you believing in me in 2020, I would not have two cookbooks under my belt now!

Sharon Hsu and Kat, NYC, 2022

So much love to all my friends and family!

Neighborhood dinner party at Kat's, 2019

About the Author

Bestselling author of *Modern Asian Baking at Home*, **Kat Lieu** is the culinary wizard behind the smash hit Subtle Asian Baking (SAB) community and a force to be reckoned with in the kitchen and beyond. Once a doctor of physical therapy, Kat's now stirring up the world of food and activism, raising dough—more than $100,000, to be exact—for various AANHPI causes, and leading the charge with The Very Asian Foundation's Creators Grant Program. Since moving into the food world, Kat has won various awards, such as the 2022 Facebook Accelerator Grant, a Pinterest Food Creator grant, and an IACP nomination for her Instagram channel. Between her feisty defenses against Internet trolls and whipping up mouthwatering masterpieces, she's battling it out in video games like *Diablo, Heroes of the Storm, Monster Hunter,* and *Overwatch*, alongside her husband and son in Seattle, Washington. And let's not forget her time spent with her adorable, food-loving shih-poo, Panda! Connect with Kat @katlieu and @subtleasian.baking and dig into her delicious world at modernasianbaking.com. You always have a seat at her table.

About the Photography Team

iida / 이다 describes the concept of being. It is a declaration of existence.

studio iida / 스튜디오 이다 is a collection of multimedia artists, material specialists, food experts, and storytellers. We are deeply curious about individual stories, how they can be felt, and how our shared experience can bring them to life through our rendition of play on materials. We respect how these stories will have their own life cycles, both in human existence and in created objects.

We create to be remembered.

studio iida, san francisco, was involved in this project. studio-iida.com

michelle min, founder and photographer. michelle@studio-iida.com

lizzie oh, founder and stylist. lizzie@studio-iida.com

Food Stylist: Selina S. Lee @selina.s.lee

Food Stylist/Assistant: Yunyi Zhang @ziraffe_z

Taiwanese Food Consultant: Linshan Huang

And a special thanks to **Nico Rasic** for introducing us to Kat's world.

Index